"This is an extremely valuable book. It is written with clarity and conviction and rooted in the author's lifelong effort to live a life true to the radical demands of the Sermon on the Mount. Filled with fresh insights and hard-earned wisdom and in dialogue with key scholarship, *Living the Sermon on the Mount in Difficult Times* will help readers to think deeper and further about this familiar text. The carefully crafted questions are particularly impressive. Designed to help individuals and groups reflect on the sermon's radical implications, they will, I am sure, prove essential to many who want to understand and respond to the challenge it poses. It is rare to find a book that will clearly transform lives. This is one of them."

—**JUSTIN MEGGITT**,
professor of the study of religion, Faculty of Divinity, University of Cambridge

"I really enjoyed reading this book. The Sermon on the Mount contains the very essence of Jesus' teachings and closely reflects how he lived his own life. However, it has often been overlooked, regarded as essentially unrealistic and irrelevant to this world. In this fascinating and much-needed book, Andrew Bolton unpacks the true meaning of the sermon and demonstrates its pertinence to the great challenges facing humanity today. I hope it will be widely read by individuals and studied within faith communities."

—**STUART MASTERS**,
author of *The Quaker Way: Friends of Love and Truth*

"What an amazing book! It inspires me to continue to grow in my new journey as a Christian in a loving community. It has motivated me through wonderful examples of the past to never give up. It has deepened my understanding of what it actually means to be a light in the darkness and reminded me that 'a thousand-mile journey begins with one step.' A really great and encouraging read!"

—**AGNETA ZUKAUSKAITE**,
young adult immigrant from Lithuania and recent Christian convert

"Andrew Bolton has been fascinated, inspired, and challenged by the Sermon on the Mount for many years. This book is the fruit of his reflections on the biblical text, its cultural context, examples of those who have lived out its teaching, and its contemporary significance. An engaging and encouraging exploration of a central Christian text."

—**STUART MURRAY-WILLIAMS,**
author of *The Naked Anabaptist*

Living the Sermon on the Mount in Difficult Times

Living the Sermon on the Mount in Difficult Times

ANDREW BOLTON

CASCADE *Books* • Eugene, Oregon

LIVING THE SERMON ON THE MOUNT IN DIFFICULT TIMES

Copyright © 2025 Andrew Bolton. All rights reserved. Except for brief quotations in critical publications or reviews, no part of this book may be reproduced in any manner without prior written permission from the publisher. Write: Permissions, Wipf and Stock Publishers, 199 W. 8th Ave., Suite 3, Eugene, OR 97401.

Cascade Books
An Imprint of Wipf and Stock Publishers
199 W. 8th Ave., Suite 3
Eugene, OR 97401

www.wipfandstock.com

PAPERBACK ISBN: 978-1-6667-5930-3
HARDCOVER ISBN: 978-1-6667-5931-0
EBOOK ISBN: 978-1-6667-5932-7

Cataloguing-in-Publication data:

Names: Bolton, Andrew, author.

Title: Living the Sermon on the Mount in difficult times / Andrew Bolton.

Description: Eugene, OR: Cascade Books, 2025 | Includes bibliographical references and index.

Identifiers: ISBN 978-1-6667-5930-3 (paperback) | ISBN 978-1-6667-5931-0 (hardcover) | ISBN 978-1-6667-5932-7 (ebook)

Subjects: LCSH: Sermon on the Mount—Criticism, interpretation, etc. | Christian ethics—Biblical teaching.

Classification: BT380.2 B65 2025 (paperback) | BT380.2 (ebook)

VERSION NUMBER 09/22/25

Unless otherwise indicated all Bible references are from the New Revised Standard Version Bible, copyright © 1989 National Council of Churches of Christ in the United States of America. Used by permission. All rights reserved worldwide.

Some material in this book is drawn from an earlier work by the author, titled *Sermon on the Mount: Foundations for an International Peace Church* (ISBN 0-8309-0834X), available at www.heraldhouse.org. This material is used with permission from Herald Publishing House and Community of Christ. All rights reserved.

For Carson Breay and Shiloh Blake
and for the blessing of all little ones

Contents

Preface: Beginning Times—Discovering the Sermon on the Mount | xi

Acknowledgments | xv

PART ONE   DIFFICULT ROMAN TIMES

1. Jesus' Times: The Roman Empire, God's Empire, Disciples, and Crucifixion | 5
2. Matthew's Roman Times: An Introduction to the Sermon on the Mount | 11

PART TWO   MEDITATIONS ON THE SERMON ON THE MOUNT

3. Living the Beatitudes | 21
4. Salt, Light, a City on a Hill | 29
5. Jesus Affirms the Law and the Prophets | 35
6. Six Discipleship Commandments | 42
7. Discipleship Commandment 1: Reconcile! | 48
8. Discipleship Commandment 2: Deal with Lust! | 53
9. Discipleship Commandment 3: Honor Marriage! | 56
10. Discipleship Commandment 4: Tell the Truth! | 61
11. Discipleship Commandment 5: No Retaliation! | 66
12. Discipleship Commandment 6: Love Your Enemies! | 72
13. Six Discipleship Commandments: Some Conclusions | 78
14. Not Showing Off and Authentic Prayer | 81
15. What is Your Heart Set On? | 88

16	Serving Two Masters and Facing Worry	92
17	Judging Others	98
18	Ask, Search, Knock!	103
19	The Golden Rule—A Basis for a Global Ethic?	108
20	Decision!	113
21	After Words: Authority and Healing	117

PART THREE LIVING THE SERMON ON THE MOUNT IN DIFFICULT TIMES

22	Early Christian Times and Living the Sermon on the Mount	125
23	Christendom Times: Fusion of Christianity with Empire	129
24	Protestant Times: Christendom Continued	135
25	Protestant Times: Dissenter Protest and Nonconformity	141
26	Colonizing Times: Exporting Christendom in European Empires	148
27	Freedom Times: Gandhi, King, and Chávez	154
28	World War I Times: The War to End All Wars?	161
29	Nazi Times: Courage in the Terror—Le Chambon and Bonhoeffer	168
30	Christian Realism Times: Niebuhr and Hauerwas	174
31	Now Times: The Possibilities of a New Christian Realism	181
32	Extraordinary Times: Polycrisis	186

Bibliography | 193

Preface

*Beginning Times—Discovering
the Sermon on the Mount*

With my three brothers, I grew up in difficult times. We lost our farm when I was eight—we were cheated by the person holding the mortgage. To cope with the shame and brokenness of the farm failing, Dad went out drinking on Tuesdays and Fridays. He came home angry, sarcastic at best, occasionally violent to us boys, although he did not hit my mother. As I was the eldest son, my mother leaned on me, but she was also strong. We owe her a debt for keeping us all together in very stressful times. All I could do was listen and pray for God to make my dad better. When I was thirteen, on a Tuesday in March, Dad came home sober. The same thing happened on the Friday, and so on. Dad stopped drinking and became a real dad.

When I was sixteen, I overheard Dad talking quietly with my mother about his visit to the family doctor that day. Dr. Lord had been injured in the D-Day landings in World War II. Dad had been a soldier for seven years in the same war. They had talked about the war. Dr. Lord understood my dad, and was also a healer. For the first time I understood that much of the pain in our family growing up was because of Dad's trauma of war. Up to that time I had romanticized war, eagerly played war games with my brothers, read avidly stories of war heroes in our comics. But from that moment on I was suspicious about war. Eventually, I discovered the Sermon on the Mount and found a comprehensively better way, that one day, when fully lived, will mean no child would be traumatized by war, poverty, or exclusion. This is how my journey with the Sermon on the Mount began. It was a response to the pain of war in our family.

Preface

The Sermon on the Mount is just 111 verses in three chapters in Matthew's Gospel. This teaching is made for memorizing and remembering. Teaching points are often organized in threes. It has repeating phrases like "Blessed are . . ." It is designed to get under our skin, into our hearts and minds, and make us ponder. Then to do, to act, to turn the world upside down.

Jesus taught in synagogues, to crowds, and in encounters with individuals. He often taught in the open air. My wife Jewell and I have sat on the Mount of Beatitudes overlooking Lake Galilee at the northern end—the site by tradition where Jesus is said to have taught the Sermon on the Mount. Together we read out loud the whole Sermon on the Mount and imagined we were there 2,000 years ago. Lake Galilee is inspiringly beautiful.

It is helpful for me to remember Jesus was a carpenter and understood apprenticeship, learning on the job. Being with Jesus for three years was not a degree course, but an apprenticeship. Two of my brothers did an apprenticeship. I trained as a horticulturalist—a posh word for gardener. I studied a lot of science, but it was applied science. The Sermon on the Mount is a key component of being an apprentice of Jesus, and it is applied Scripture. Jesus taught his disciples how to understand the Torah and the Prophets. Then how they applied it was up to them.[1] In their partnership with Jesus the disciples were to be creative, also craftspeople, with initiative. So you too are invited to practice, experiment, and be creative with the principles that you learn in these 111 verses. Gandhi, who read the Sermon on the Mount every day for forty years, called his autobiography *The Story of My Experiments with Truth*.

This book is an introduction to the Sermon on the Mount and can be read by yourself. It can also be used for group study on a Sunday morning, or some other time during the week. The first time Jesus taught these sayings, it was with a small group of disciples, with a crowd listening in. The Sermon on the Mount was taught out loud in the early church because most people could not read. The Sermon on the Mount is personal, but it is for living in fellowship, community. Plural words like "theirs," "those," and "they" are used. The Lord's Prayer begins with "*Our* Father . . ."

Jesus is a typical rabbi encouraging questions from his student-apprentices, and the Gospels report the back-and-forth conversations. To help your back-and-forth conversations, there are discussion questions throughout this book. Let your prayer at the beginning and end of each

---

1. Betz and Schweiker, "Concerning Mountains and Morals," 17.

Preface

study be to invite the Spirit of Jesus to illuminate these words in your mind and heart.

So much has been written on the Sermon on the Mount. So much continues to be written. It is impossible to read all the excellent work by scholars and those who practice and live the Sermon on the Mount. This book is just an introduction and it is written for ordinary people. I try to follow John Wesley's example and make things simple. Do not be put off or distracted by all the footnotes. These are there because I want to thank those I have read and who have helped me by giving them due scholarly recognition. The footnotes are there also to enable you to follow up something of interest if you want to.

To understand "difficult times" also has meant reading history. This book is a brief introduction to some Christian history, and thus often partial. I readily confess that my reading and writing about history has a bias. I want to understand history from the point of view of the victims of violence and poverty. To see history from the cross, rather than from the point of view of Caesar, Herod, Pilate, or Winston Churchill. Violence has served Roman, European, and American empires well, but crucified their victims.

This text seeks to feminize and decolonize the debate as to whether the Sermon on the Mount is relevant today. It then asks how relevant is the just war tradition and Christian realism for addressing the big human security questions of the twenty-first century: climate change, the widening gap between rich and poor, mass migration, racism, populism, and nuclear weapons. Learning from the past, can we begin together to develop a new, robust Christian realism, that takes seriously the Sermon on the Mount, and finds in it a way of salvation for our own difficult, poly-crisis times? Some Christians are already doing this and I cite some of them.

Exemplars are given of peace and justice makers without suggesting any individual is a perfect saint or peacemaker. Gandhi, Martin Luther King Jr., John Howard Yoder, and John Wesley, for example, are mentioned with respect, but they are also flawed and I want to acknowledge this candidly. The Bible is very realistic about human failings, but it also tells redemption stories. We do not have to be perfect to make a contribution to the work of the Divine. Without excusing or condoning any failure, there is thus hope for all of us; all of us can make a contribution to a greater peace.

You are invited to bring an alert, open, and hopeful mind to the study of the Sermon on the Mount. This book is not a dogmatic last word, but is intended to help in important continuing conversions. Equipped with the

Preface

Sermon on the Mount, and loving God with our all, our task with Jesus and other disciples is to change the world. No child should go to bed hungry, be terrorized by war or violence, or have to face massive climate change.

Andrew Bolton
Easter, 2025
Leicester, England

Acknowledgments

This book would not have been published without the support of Stuart Murray Williams of the British Anabaptist Network.

There is a vast ocean of scholarship on the Sermon on the Mount—books, academic papers, and so on. This book is simply an introduction, and I am grateful for conversations with four New Testament scholars: Lloyd Pietersen, Bristol Baptist College, UK; Mark Bredin, a British Quaker; Dorothy Jean Weaver, Eastern Mennonite Seminary, Virginia; and Dan Ulrich, Bethany Seminary, Indiana. Lloyd Pietersen was particularly helpful in graciously sending PDF copies of papers he was recommending. These scholars were a joy to talk to. I am grateful for their guidance but fully acknowledge that any shortcomings in this book are mine.

I thank readers Mike Botts, Miles Hillmann, Pauline Holmes, Rachel Pepa, Will Smith, Stuart Murray Williams, Zachary Weaver-Shojaie, Ian Wilson, Mike Young, and Agneta Zukauskaite. They gave me encouragement, pointed out problems, and reduced my potential embarrassment with mistakes. I also thank Matt Frizzell, David Howlett, and Elray Henriksen for suggestions of books and papers, and in particular our many conversations on peace studies and nonviolence.[2] Conversations with consultant clinical psychologist and lay minister, Dr. James Rathbone, exploring the possible psychology of Jesus' teachings, have been illuminating.

Rodney Clapp has been a consistently encouraging editor from Wipf and Stock.

---

2. How to spell *nonviolence*? Should it be non-violence, or simply nonviolence without the hyphen? See King, "Why We Need Sharp's Dictionary." King states: "Yet even in English, something so small as the decision to hyphenate—nonviolent and nonviolence versus non-violent and non-violence—is ambiguous. Hyphenating the expression further accentuates a negative connotation; without a hyphen, the word becomes a more straightforward affirmation." I thus choose nonviolence without the hyphen.

Acknowledgments

My first book on the Sermon on the Mount was published in 1999. It was a brief Sunday school introduction. Although this latest volume is much longer, and benefits from twenty-five years more reading and working on the Sermon on the Mount, some ideas, phrases, and passages continue in this volume. I am grateful for permission from Herald House and Community of Christ for being able to use some of this content.

Finally, Jewell is my spouse of nearly fifty years. She creatively, lovingly, and sometimes boldly embodies the Sermon on the Mount in our relationship. I am grateful for her companionship.

"The Sermon on the Mount is the constitution of the Kingdom of God, the Magna Carta of Christianity."

—MARIAN MACHINEK, POLAND[1]

The Sermon on the Mount "presents the perfect, unadulterated will of God, the will of God in its nakedness, because it proclaims the will of God as it should be lived in the kingdom. This explains why it is seemingly heedless of all earthly contingencies, why it is so radical, why it will always blast complacency and shallow moralism, disturb every good conscience and instil terror in those who take it seriously."

—W. D. DAVIES AND DALE C. ALLISON JR., WALES/USA[2]

"The Sermon on the Mount is undoubtedly the most well-known, celebrated and provocative speech in human history. No other famous oration posed a more thoroughgoing challenge to every generation, its religious life, its politics, its everyday ethos."

—ANDRIE B. DU TOIT, SOUTH AFRICA[3]

"If Jesus really walked upon the earth, why do we keep treating him as if he were a disembodied, impossible idealistic theory? If he was a real man, then the Sermon on the Mount was made for people on this earth; and if he existed, God has shown us in flesh and blood what good is for flesh-and-blood people."

—ANDRÉ TROCMÉ, FRANCE[4]

---

1. Machinek, "Gerhard Lohfink's Interpretative Key," 1336.
2. Davies and Allison Jr., "Reflections on the Sermon on the Mount," 304.
3. Du Toit, "Revisiting the Sermon on the Mount," 60.
4. Cited in Hallie, *Lest Innocent Blood*, 68.

"When Christian interpreters emphasised the 'impossibility' of the Sermon, Gandhi showed its practicality in the affairs of real life. For example, many theologians contended that the Sermon on the Mount does not apply to mundane things and ordinary people, and that it was only meant for the twelve disciples. To this Gandhi replied: 'Well, I do not believe this. I think the Sermon on the Mount has no meaning if it is not of vital use in everyday life to everyone.'"

—P. T. SUBRAHMANYAN, INDIA[5]

"It is NOT much of an exaggeration to say that Christian ethics consists of a series of footnotes to the Sermon on the Mount."

—GARRETT E. PAUL, USA[6]

"Jesus embodies the Sermon on the Mount, and invites us to do the same."

—SOURCE UNKNOWN

---

5. Subrahmanyan, "Mahatma Gandhi," 4–5.
6. Paul, "Jesus' Ethic of Perfection," 270.

PART ONE

Difficult Roman Times

1

Jesus' Times

*The Roman Empire, God's Empire,
Disciples, and Crucifixion*

> When Herod saw that he had been tricked by the wise men he was infuriated, and he sent and killed all the children in and around Bethlehem who were two years old or under . . . (Matthew 2:16)

> So [Pilate] released Barabbas for them; and after flogging Jesus, he handed him over to be crucified. (Matthew 27:26)

JESUS AND DIFFICULT ROMAN TIMES

Matthew's Gospel is a witness to difficult Roman times. Matthew, placed at the very start of the New Testament, begins with the context of the Roman Empire and its collaborators. To understand Jesus, Matthew would have us understand Rome.

Jesus was born, ministered, and died in difficult Roman times. He proclaimed that God's upside-down empire was good news and much better than Caesar's empire. In difficult times the Sermon on the Mount can be considered as the constitution of God's coming reign for disciples yesterday and today.

King Herod the Great, a client king of the Roman Empire, ruled Judea from Jerusalem. In a paranoid rage, after hearing from the magi that the king of the Jews had been born, he slaughtered all the baby boys under two

Part One | Difficult Roman Times

in the Bethlehem area, near the time of Jesus' birth.[1] Jesus and his parents fled as refugees to Egypt.[2] Later John the Baptist, a relative of Jesus, was arrested by Herod the Great's son, Herod Antipas, the tetrarch, after John had criticized Antipas publicly for marrying his brother's wife. Later, Herod had John beheaded.[3] After Jesus cleansed the temple for charging outrageous prices for sacrificial animals to the pious poor, the chief priests and scribes looked for a way to kill him "by stealth."[4] Betrayed by Judas, arrested, tried, and found guilty by the Jewish Sanhedrin, Jesus was delivered to Roman governor Pilate for crucifixion by Roman soldiers.[5]

If you want a fast-paced, well-written account of the Roman Empire read Tom Holland's *Rubicon: The Triumph and Tragedy of the Roman Republic*.

But for now, what is important to know about Rome and its empire as the context for Jesus' times and as background for Matthew's Gospel?

First of all, the Jerusalem temple stood not only at the heart of the local economy, but it was "also politically central to the whole political economy of the Roman province of Judea."[6] The high priestly and ruling Herodian families benefited from collaborating with the Romans with wealth, privilege, and power. They profited from the temple as a religious business enabling the forgiveness of sins. The Romans kept them in that advantageous business position.

Second, the Romans were ruthless. They destroyed Carthage in 146 BCE and Corinth around the same time. Pompey marched into Syria and Mesopotamia in 64–63 BCE, and Palestine was one of the last corners of the Mediterranean world to be taken over by the Romans. The Roman new world order brought power and privilege to the Roman elite, and glory to Rome. Subject people, peasants generating agricultural wealth, experienced *Pax Romana* as a "disruptive, disorientating, or even devastating new world disorder."[7]

Roman collaborators were also ruthless. King Herod the Great (reigned 37 BCE–c. 4 BCE) taxed severely on behalf of the Romans, and

1. Matthew 2:16.
2. Matthew 2:13–15.
3. Matthew 14:1–12.
4. Matthew 21:12–13, 26:3–5; Mark 11:18–19; Luke 19:45–47.
5. Matthew 26:47—27:44.
6. Horsley, *Jesus and Empire*, 10.
7. Horsley, *Jesus and Empire*, 21.

also took a further cut to support his extravagant building projects. Thus, there were three layers of economic exploitation: (1) temple tithes (2) taxes to support Herod (3) and tax tribute to Rome.[8] It was a crushing burden for Jewish peasants. No wonder tax collectors get bad press in the Gospels. Herod Antipas, Herod the Great's son, ruled over Galilee and Perea 1–39 CE, and wastefully built two capitals in this small province. Living in Galilee, his extraction of taxes was efficient and severe. This created crises in the families and villages in Galilee, particularly in bad harvest years when farmers went into debt to feed their children, and then would lose their land when unable to repay their loans.

Third, the Roman Empire was supported by an imperial and militaristic ideology. This was reinforced by the cult of the emperor who was hailed as divine, worshipped as a savior, and celebrated by shrines in public places throughout the Roman world. Subject peoples were also forced to worship the Roman army standards. Pontius Pilate, even though he knew Jewish beliefs about graven images, introduced effigies or sculptures of Caesar into Jerusalem by night.[9] Part of the drive for imperial expansion came from having to feed in Rome a population of more than a million people. Rome was filled with displaced and impoverished peasants who had lost their land while fighting in Roman legions. Bread and circuses were important to keep the population in Rome pacified.[10]

To keep subject peoples in their place and still paying taxes, the Romans used "crucifixion, mass slaughter, enslavement, and massacres of whole towns, and annihilation of whole peoples" in order to terrorize them into submission.[11]

Despite brutal Roman repression, Jewish peasants were among the most difficult in the Roman Empire to rule. Inspired by the story of the Exodus, of how God had delivered Hebrew slaves from the tyrant Pharaoh, desperate peasant Jews believed God could help them find military victory over the Romans. One revolt was in Galilee 4 BCE, around the time Jesus was born. In the area near Nazareth 2,000 men were crucified in punishment and to intimidate the Galileans. It must have traumatized a whole generation, among whom Jesus grew up.[12] In the 50s CE,

---

8. Horsley, *Jesus and Empire*, 32.
9. Horsley, *Jesus and Empire*, 22–23, 31.
10. Horsley, *Jesus and Empire*, 24–25.
11. Horsley, *Jesus and Empire*, 27.
12. Horsley, *Jesus and Empire*, 28–30.

a group called the Sicarii, or daggermen, arose. In crowded Jerusalem streets they would assassinate Romans or Jewish collaborators.[13] This was counterterrorism in response to the terrorism of Roman rule. In the great revolt of 66–70 CE, the Romans laid siege to Jerusalem and crucified 500 people every day in full sight of the walls around the city.[14] The temple was destroyed and Jerusalem laid to waste. The Kitos War, 115–117 CE, saw another Jewish revolt, although fought largely outside Judea. The Bar Kokhba revolt of 132–136 CE was the last major revolt. The Jews were initially successful, but the Romans finally gained the upper hand through overwhelming force. Nearly 600,000 Jews were killed, many more died from disease and hunger, whole areas were depopulated, and captives were again sold into slavery. Afterwards Jews were barred from living in, or entering, Jerusalem.

It appears that Christians did not revolt. For one thing they were not attached to a land, but spread throughout the Roman Empire, and often lived dispersed in cities. Nevertheless, from the crucifixion of Jesus onwards, they suffered sporadic persecution in the Roman Empire for the first 300 years of the church, and many were martyred. It was Jesus' teachings in the Sermon on the Mount that were important in the formation of new Christians, and that also guided the patient response of the early Christians to Roman brutality and persecution. This was a successful strategy, for the early Christians did not provoke further repression by retaliation. Many converts were attracted by the early Christians' courageous, ethical, and loving witness, and the church grew.[15]

So, the colonizing Roman world of imperial violence and taxation was the context in which Jesus grew up and performed his ministry. Jesus from Nazareth fully shared in the suffering and trauma of his people. When Jesus went throughout Galilee "proclaiming the good news of the kingdom,"[16] it was also in judgement of the Roman Empire. This was the context for the first teaching of the Sermon on the Mount. For a people who felt cursed

---

13. Horsley, *Jesus and Empire*, 42–43.

14. Horsley, *Jesus and Empire*, 29. Horsley cites the Jewish historian Josephus, who does not specify how many days these mass crucifixions lasted.

15. See Kreider, *Patient Ferment*. Kreider documents and elucidates wonderfully the long discipleship formation processes of the early Christians, the centrality of the Sermon on the Mount's teachings, and new habits developed by converts of serving the poor, humility, and a reconciling communal life.

16. Matthew 4:23.

by Roman occupation, Jesus' teachings begins with eight blessings—the Beatitudes. God's way was good news, even if Herod and Caesar were not.

Sometimes the Sermon on the Mount is dismissed as too idealistic and impractical in a violent, oppressive, real world. However, Matthew's Gospel is not at all naive about the violence, oppression, and colonialism of the Roman Empire. He describes it in vivid detail. In addition, the Sermon on the Mount was important in the flourishing early church for the first 300 years; it was taught and lived by persecuted early Christians living mostly in the Roman world. Thus, neither can it be said that the early Christians were naive about the violence and oppression in the real world of the Roman Empire. They lived and suffered it every day.

The Sermon on the Mount was taught and valued by those who lived in very difficult Roman times in the early church, and the church not only survived, it grew.

REFLECTIONS

1. Imagine you and your family lived in Galilee at the time of Jesus. Today we often complain about our government and its policies. What would you be saying with family and neighbors about King Herod and his government in the privacy of your own home? If Jesus joined your conversation as a young adult, what might he say?
2. In Galilee, when you saw a soldier, what thoughts might go through your head? To what extent does he represent freedom, security, or safety for you and your family? Or does his presence frustrate these things? Where in the world today are people suffering from official violence serving law and order?
3. Imagine you are an early Christian living in Antioch, Alexandria, or Rome. How might times have been difficult for you? Are you realistic or naïve about your own situation in society?

Prayer thought

Thank you, God, that in Jesus you entered fully and vulnerably into our hurting, traumatized world. Help us remember those that suffer violence today, and be part of their relief and advocacy. We pray for conversion of our own hearts and also of those in power. Amen.

2

Matthew's Roman Times

An Introduction to the Sermon on the Mount

COMMENTARIES

There is an ocean of literature on the Sermon on the Mount. So, it is helpful to know first of all the best scholarly commentaries to refer to.

Welsh Congregational minister and later American academic W. D. Davies, with American scholar D. C. Allison Jr., wrote *A Critical and Exegetical Commentary on the Gospel According to St. Matthew*. This is a three-volume work. The Sermon on the Mount is covered in the first volume. They present with care, clarity, and nuance from a large range of scholarship, and their own work on Matthew.

Swiss academic Ulrich Luz wrote a four-volume commentary on Matthew's Gospel that was first published in 1985. In 2007 a fresh English translation of the German fifth edition was published as a three-volume work. The Sermon on the Mount is covered in the first volume: *Matthew 1–7*. (Hermeneia: a *Critical and Historical Commentary on the Bible*). Dale C. Allison Jr., scholarly partner of W. D. Davies above, has stated that Ulrich Luz was perhaps the best scholar on the Gospel of Matthew in the world.[1]

German-American scholar Hans Dieter Betz's commentary *The Sermon on the Mount* also includes the Sermon on the Plain in the Gospel of Luke. This monumental work of 695 pages was published in 1995.

---

1. Allison Jr., "Ulrich Luz, *Matthew 1–7*," 133.

The above three commentaries are comprehensive, encyclopedic, and great to consult, but probably best borrowed from a library since they are expensive. New Zealander Baptist Warren Carter, now working in the US, is an interesting contrast. He wrote an affordable one-volume commentary called *Matthew and the Margins: A Sociopolitical and Religious Reading*. He reads Matthew in terms of its social, political, and religious context. He argues that the congregation Matthew originally wrote for was on the social margins of the city they lived in. Carter suggests that middle-class scholars in Western universities might miss this perspective.

Carter is not the only one to write on Matthew with a perspective from the margins. For example Mark Bredin does so too in his recent book on Matthew's Gospel, *Jesus, Revolutionary of the Poor*.[2] A Quaker, he is informed by his work with people struggling on the margins today: those with learning difficulties, the poor in Zimbabwe and East Africa, the homeless, and those struggling with mental health issues.[3] Mennonite Dorothy Jean Weaver wrote *The Irony of Power: The Politics of God within Matthew's Narrative*. She writes from what she calls her 3-M perspective: her Mennonite commitment, her academic work on Matthew's Gospel, and her engagement in the Middle East in the occupied Palestinian territories. She sees the ancient and contemporary world as one "afflicted by brutality, violence, injustice, and oppression . . . where powerful people were on top and powerless people were on the bottom."[4]

THE TEXT AND BACKGROUND OF MATTHEW

Davies and Allison state at the beginning of their commentary: "Context defines meaning, and if our Gospel text is the foreground, then it cannot be placed in perspective without its background."[5]

Foreground: The Story in Matthew

First, consider the foreground in summary. The Sermon on the Mount has to be read as a part of the whole Gospel of Matthew. It is the first training

---

2. Bredin, *Jesus, Revolutionary of the Poor*.
3. Bredin, *Jesus, Revolutionary of the Poor*, 7.
4. Weaver, *Irony of Power*, xv.
5. Davies and Allison Jr., *Matthew 1–7*, 6.

session for the first disciples, Peter and Andrew, James and John, with a sympathetic crowd of seekers listening in. It is preceded by Jesus' baptism, his three temptations, and then Jesus going into Galilee proclaiming the arrival of the kingdom of God, not as a soldier, but as a teacher and healer.[6] Jesus begins with acts of unconditional grace through his healing ministry. Then comes the Sermon on the Mount as teaching on basic discipleship in 111 verses in Matthew chapters 5–7. It is immediately followed by three healing stories: a leper, the servant of a Roman centurion, and Peter's mother-in-law.[7] Thus teaching on discipleship is preceded and followed by deeds of grace by Jesus.[8] Healing is generously and compassionately extended to all, even a servant of an officer of the hated Roman occupying army. Bands of courageous missionary disciples will heal first Israel,[9] and then the world, by living the Sermon on the Mount. The Great Commission, the last instruction to the disciples by Jesus, is to "make disciples of all nations, baptising them . . . and teaching them to obey everything that I have commanded you."[10] This of course includes the Sermon on the Mount.

Background of Matthew's Gospel

Context of the Roman Empire

Jesus was born into a violent, Roman-controlled world, and this story is told vividly in Matthew from the beginning to the end of the Gospel—from the birth of Jesus and the killing of all the baby boys around Bethlehem, to the crucifixion of Jesus. The context of the Roman Empire has already been described in the previous chapter.

The Author of Matthew's Gospel

The evidence is clear that the anonymous author of what we call Matthew's Gospel was a Jewish Christian, familiar with rabbinic methods, and who grew up bilingual or trilingual (speaking Greek, Hebrew, and Aramaic).[11]

6. Matthew 3:13–17; 4:1–25.
7. Matthew 8:1–15.
8. Luz, *Matthew 1–7*, 10.
9. Matthew 10: 1–8.
10. Matthew 28:19–20.
11. Davies and Allison Jr., *Matthew 1–7*, 33, 58, 73.

It was an early Christian tradition that the author was the apostle Matthew, but Davies and Allison question this.[12] What is beyond doubt is that the author is inclusive of both fellow Jews and gentiles. This Gospel "breathes a Jewish atmosphere and yet looks upon the Gentile mission in a most favourable light."[13] The mission field is the whole world.[14] Church and synagogue are not yet divided, and Matthew's criticisms are directed at Jewish leaders, not the Jewish people.

The Structure and Sources of Matthew's Gospel

The basic structure of Matthew's Gospel consists of five blocks of teaching, interspersed with stories of Jesus. The five blocks of teaching echo the first five books of the Bible from Genesis to Deuteronomy—the Torah. In them Jesus teaches the ethics of the kingdom. This structure suggests Jesus is a new Moses who has revealed a new Torah.[15] The first and longest of these five blocks is the Sermon on the Mount, Matthew chapters 5–7.

It is thought that these five blocks of teaching were drawn from an early, now lost, document called Q, named after the German word *Quelle* for spring or source. Q contained sayings of Jesus and is the basis of the Sermon on the Mount.[16] The other major source used by Matthew is the Gospel of Mark. Thus, ethical teaching is combined with the story of Jesus. Matthew's Gospel of the kingdom is a grace story. Grace is why it is good news. Ulrich Luz puts it this way: "[Matthew] joined Jesus' ethical proclamation of the kingdom of God to the story of God's activity with Jesus, thus making it the proclamation of grace."[17]

In addition, Matthew often thinks in threes or triads. Jesus suffers three temptations, for example. The Sermon on the Mount itself is packed full of other triads.[18] For example, Jesus' teachings on anger, lust, divorce, oath-making, retaliation, and loving enemies in Matthew 5:21–48 are structured into two triads. In chapter 6 there is another triplet: almsgiving, prayer, and fasting. If you take out the Lord's Prayer of this section, the

---

12. Davies and Allison Jr., *Matthew 1–7*, 14, 17.
13. Davies and Allison Jr., *Matthew 1–7*, 144.
14. Davies and Allison Jr., *Matthew 1–7*, 23–24. Matthew 28:19–20.
15. Davies and Allison Jr., *Matthew 1–7*, 59, 61. Luz, *Matthew 1–7*, 13.
16. See for instance Kloppenborg, *Q, the Earliest Gospel*.
17. Luz, *Matthew 1–7*, 12–13.
18. Davies and Allison Jr., *Matthew 1–7*, 62–64.

number of words for these three themes is sixty-four, sixty-five, and sixty-three, almost identical.[19]

The Lord's Prayer begins with three petitions to "Our Father" (hallowed be your name, your kingdom come, your will be done), and then three petitions for human need (daily bread, forgiveness of debts, do not bring us to the time of trial).[20] Glen Stassen and others take this triadic structure further, and more on Stassen's work will be shared later.

There are also other patterns in the Sermon on the Mount. Mark Bredin, for instance, points out that the eight Beatitudes can be divided into four plus four, each set with thirty-six words in the Greek text.[21] More can be said about the structure of the Sermon on the Mount, but this is enough to indicate how the writer of Matthew has thoughtfully structured this first block of teachings by Jesus.

Although not poetry, the Sermon on the Mount is as creatively crafted as any great poem. To glimpse this is to come near a great mind and soul who loved being a disciple of Jesus and wanted others to enter into the joy and calling of this way. The word pictures of Jesus' teachings are beautifully and carefully framed.

Audience, When and Where?

The Sermon on the Mount describes two audiences: the inner circle of committed disciples, and then an outer circle of the crowd, open, curious, wanting to know more.[22] Perhaps we would today call the crowd "seekers." They came from Galilee, the Decapolis, Jerusalem, Judea, and beyond Jordan[23]—from Israel, which is Jesus' first focus for missionary work.[24] A third audience is named at the end of Matthew's Gospel: "all nations"—to which the first apostles are sent to make disciples, baptize, and teach everything that Jesus has commanded.[25] A fourth audience is the congregation of Jewish Christians that Matthew first wrote for, near the end of the first century,

---

19. Du Toit, "Revisiting the Sermon on the Mount," 86.
20. Du Toit, "Revisiting the Sermon on the Mount," 87.
21. Bredin, *Jesus, Revolutionary of the Poor*, 142.
22. Matthew 5:1.
23. Matthew 4:25.
24. Matthew 10:5–6.
25. Matthew 28:19–20.

a congregation that also embraced gentiles. A fifth audience is you and me today.

Davies and Allison argue that Matthew was probably written in Antioch, but this is more a best guess than a definite conclusion.[26] They suggest it was written between 70–100 CE, and probably 80–95 CE.[27] Again it is after the Jewish Revolt of 66–70 CE.

Warren Carter agrees that Matthew's Gospel was written for a congregation in Antioch, Syria—a small, marginal group of Jewish Christians.[28] Syria is mentioned in the four Gospels only once—in Matthew.[29] Carter argues persuasively for this city, as do some others,[30] although other scholars leave it open, simply as a city in Israel. Carter states that if it was not Antioch, then his further arguments still hold. The advantage of thinking about Antioch is that it helps us have a definite place to understand the likely first audience that heard Matthew's Gospel.

If Matthew was writing for a marginal group in Antioch nearly 2,000 years ago, what does marginal mean for Carter? It means being on the edge, even an outsider. Marginal is the opposite of being part of the in-crowd religiously, ideologically, or economically. Matthew's Christians in Antioch do not live as the wealthy and the powerful. They are not in control of the city. The early Christians in Antioch were nonconformists, quietly resisting the pressures of the Roman Empire, and also at odds with the larger Jewish community. Thus, Carter reads Matthew's Gospel as a counter-narrative, a contrary story, that is resisting "male above female, king above people, ruler above ruled, rich above poor, religious leaders above people, violence above compassion, the center above the margins."[31] Carter goes on to say, "The Gospel reveals that Rome's Empire is doomed."[32]

Matthew's central purpose is to tell a story that strengthens the identity and discipleship lifestyle of the Antioch congregation.[33] Antioch was big

26. Davies and Allison Jr., *Matthew 1–7*, 146–47.
27. Davies and Allison Jr., *Matthew 1–7*, 138.
28. Carter, *Matthew and the Margins*, 15–16.
29. Matthew 4:24.
30. Du Toit, "Revisiting the Sermon on the Mount," 62–63. Du Toit quotes scholarly authorities such as Werner Kummel, Robert Gundry, Ulrich Luz, and Bart Ehrman, who support Antioch as the location for the first audience of Matthew's Gospel. As already mentioned Davies and Allison Jr. also lean towards Antioch.
31. Carter, *Matthew and the Margins*, 1–3.
32. Carter, *Matthew and the Margins*, 4.
33. Carter, *Matthew and the Margins*, 8–11.

in first-century terms, perhaps the third largest city in the Roman Empire, after Rome and Alexandria in Egypt. Its population was maybe 150,000 to 200,000, and it was densely populated. The city and the surrounding countryside were structured hierarchically, with mutual hostility between the elite and the non-elite. To keep the peace of Rome, *Pax Romana*, violence was used; peace was enforced through bloodshed.[34]

Existence for the non-elite was difficult and miserable. Carter quotes American sociologist Rodney Stark's description of Antioch:

> Any accurate picture of Antioch in New Testament times must depict a city filled with misery, danger, fear, despair and hatred. Antioch was a city where the average family lived a squalid life in filthy and cramped quarters, where at least half of the children died at birth or during infancy ... The city was filled with hatred and fear rooted in intense ethnic antagonisms ... Crime flourished ... Antioch was repeatedly smashed by cataclysmic catastrophes.[35]

It seems probable that the Christian community in Antioch was a cross-section of the city's population, without those at the very top or utter bottom.[36] It is evident that there is practical compassion for the bottom, as Matthew has Jesus saying in the final judgement parable:

> For I was hungry and you gave me food, I was thirsty and you gave me something to drink, I was a stranger and you welcomed me, I was naked and you gave me clothing, I was sick and you took care of me, I was in prison and you visited me.[37]

How large was this Antioch Christian congregation? Rodney Stark estimates that in the year 100 there were perhaps just 7,530 Christians in the whole Roman Empire. In Antioch the congregation could have been as small as nineteen, or as large as 150, or even a thousand disciples.[38]

The Sermon on the Mount, as the largest teaching block in Matthew's Gospel, helped shape an alternative Christian identity and communal life that was effective resistance to the violence, exploitation, poverty, and corruption of the Roman Empire.

---

34. Adapted from Carter, *Matthew and the Margins*, 18–21.
35. Stark, cited in Carter, *Matthew and the Margins*, 24.
36. Stark, cited in Carter, *Matthew and the Margins*, 25–27.
37. Matthew 25:36–37.
38. Carter, *Matthew and the Margins*, 28–29.

REFLECTIONS

1. How would congregational life in Antioch 2,000 years ago differ from and be the same as your experience of congregational life?
2. How does the background of Matthew's Gospel, for example author, date, audience, location, help us understand better the message of this gospel?
3. There is a structure to Matthew's Gospel as a whole, for instance five blocks of teaching, of which the Sermon on the Mount is the first and longest. Often a structure of threes is used in the Sermon on the Mount and throughout the Gospel. And the first four Beatitudes have exactly the same number of words as the last four Beatitudes in the original Greek. Will it be helpful to think of the Sermon on the Mount as carefully crafted as any poem as you read it? Does the literary skill and care of the author enhance this Gospel's message for you?

Prayer Thought

God of then, God of now, God of Matthew, and God of us, guide us by your Holy Spirit as we use our minds fully to understand Jesus and congregational life for early Christians in difficult times. Amen.

PART TWO

Meditations on the Sermon on the Mount

3

Living the Beatitudes

INTRODUCTION

Beatitude means blessing. The Sermon on the Mount begins with eight blessings:

> 5 ¹When Jesus saw the crowds, he went up the mountain; and after he sat down, his disciples came to him. ² Then he began to speak, and taught them, saying:
> ³ "Blessed are the poor in spirit, for theirs is the kingdom of heaven.
> ⁴ "Blessed are those who mourn, for they will be comforted.
> ⁵ "Blessed are the meek, for they will inherit the earth.
> ⁶ "Blessed are those who hunger and thirst for righteousness, for they will be filled.
> ⁷ "Blessed are the merciful, for they will receive mercy.
> ⁸ "Blessed are the pure in heart, for they will see God.
> ⁹ "Blessed are the peacemakers, for they will be called children of God.
> ¹⁰ "Blessed are those who are persecuted for righteousness' sake, for theirs is the kingdom of heaven.
> ¹¹ "Blessed are you when people revile you and persecute you and utter all kinds of evil against you falsely on my account. ¹² Rejoice and be glad, for your reward is great in heaven, for in the same way they persecuted the prophets who were before you. (Matthew 5:1–12)

Part Two | Sermon on the Mount

First Thoughts

1. What are your first thoughts about this text and its message as you read it?

2. What patterns do you see in this passage?

ANNOUNCING THE KINGDOM OF GOD

In a Roman colonial context, the central message of both John the Baptist and Jesus is the same in Matthew's Gospel: "Repent, for the kingdom of heaven has come near."[1] John's baptism, embraced by Jesus, was the baptism of repentance.[2] Reading of Jesus' baptism prepares us for hearing the Sermon on the Mount. Jesus' baptismal commitment includes rejecting three major temptations of the Roman Empire—economic power, religious power, and military power.[3] Sri Lankan theologian Peniel Rajkumar interestingly argues that the later development of the British Empire was done through a similar unholy trio of merchant, missionary, and soldier.[4] Jesus rejects these temptations, and refuses to compromise the call of the kingdom of heaven.

What does repentance mean? In Hebrew *teshuvah* means turning towards God and the right.[5] The parable of the prodigal son wonderfully describes the turning of the son.[6] The Greek word in Matthew's Gospel used for repentance is *metanoia*. It means to change your mind. Paul says this in Romans: "Do not be conformed to this world but be transformed by the renewing of your minds, so that you may discern what is the will of God—what is good and acceptable and perfect."[7]

1. Matthew 3:2; 4:17.
2. Matthew 3:11.
3. Matthew 4:1–11.
4. Rajkumar, "Postcolonialism," 104.
5. My Jewish Learning, "Teshuvah, or Repentance."
6. Luke 15:11–32.
7. Romans 12:2.

The author of John's Gospel has Jesus telling Nicodemus, "No one can enter the kingdom of God without being born of water and Spirit."[8] In some Christian traditions baptism by immersion and confirmation for the gift of the Holy Spirit beautifully symbolizes rebirth.

Repentance means conversion of all of life to the kingdom way. It is all of Jesus for every aspect of our life. It is rejection of Caesar, Herod, and the injustices and violence of empire.

JESUS, MOSES, AND EXODUS

The story of Moses, the greatest Jewish prophet, can be summarized as follows:

Exodus Journey				
slaughter of infants	return of hero	passage through water	temptations	mountain of lawgiving[9]

Pharaoh ordered the slaughter of baby boys, but Pharaoh's daughter rescued Moses and he grew up in Pharaoh's court.[10] He murdered an Egyptian slave driver and fled into exile. God heard the cries of the Hebrew slaves and confronted Moses in the burning bush vision.[11] After the burning bush experience, Moses was commissioned to ask Pharaoh to liberate the Hebrews slaves.[12] They escaped through a path in the sea.[13] The Hebrews in the wilderness were tempted by idolatry and doubt.[14] Moses gave them the law on Mount Sinai, including the Ten Commandments.[15]

This same sequence can be found in Matthew's telling of the story of Jesus in the first five chapters of the Gospel: slaughter of infants by King

---

8. John 3:5.
9. Allison Jr., *Sermon on the Mount*, 17–19.
10. Exodus 1:8–2:10.
11. Exodus 2:23–3:10.
12. Exodus 3:1–10; 4:18–20.
13. Exodus 14.
14. Exodus 32; Numbers 13–14; Psalm 95:10.
15. Exodus 19–20.

Herod,[16] return of the hero,[17] passage through water (baptism),[18] temptations in the wilderness,[19] and the giving of the law (Sermon on the Mount).[20]

Exodus is a central story in the Hebrew Scriptures. It is an amazing story. God is not on the side of Pharaoh, who owns Egypt, but on the side of immigrant slaves who do not even own their own bodies. And God commissions Moses to lead them to freedom.

Is exodus a significant theme in Matthew?

Jesus announces the good news of the kingdom, and then at the beginning of the Sermon on the Mount we find reference to Isaiah 61:1–2, as in Luke 4:18–19, expressed in the Beatitudes:

> Blessed are the poor in spirit, for theirs is the kingdom of heaven. (Isaiah 61:1)
> Blessed are those who mourn, for they will be comforted. (Isaiah 61:2)
> Blessed are those who hunger and thirst for righteousness, for they will be filled. (Isaiah 61:8)
> Rejoice and be glad (Isaiah 61:10)[21]

Matthew has Jesus singing the song of exodus hope, the most revolutionary story in the Hebrew Bible, but now applied in the context of Roman colonization.

It is helpful to see the Beatitudes in terms of present and future conditions:

Present condition	Future condition
poor in spirit	theirs is the kingdom
mourn	be comforted
meek	inherit the earth
hunger	be filled
merciful	receive mercy
pure in heart	see God
peacemakers	children of God
persecuted	theirs is the kingdom
persecuted for righteousness	reward is great[22]

16. Matthew 2:16–18.
17. Matthew 2:19–23.
18. Matthew 3:13–17.
19. Matthew 4:1–11.
20. Matthew 5–7.
21. See Allison Jr., *Sermon on the Mount*, 15–16.
22. See Allison Jr., *Sermon on the Mount*, 42, using NRSV translation.

Living the Beatitudes

Exodus to the promised land flowing with milk and honey is coming.

As already mentioned, Mark Bredin sees the eight Beatitudes as four plus four.[23] The first four Beatitudes are blessings for victims of poverty, the grief stricken, those suffering humiliation and injustice. Bredin argues that the first Beatitude, "Blessed are the poor in spirit," is not Matthew spiritualizing poverty, but really means "*the very poorest of the poor*," those who have no reason to hope. The fourth Beatitude, "Blessed are those who hunger and thirst for justice," means those who are literally hungry and thirsty, suffering the injustice of terrible, aching poverty.[24] Their desperate conditions are going to end. Exodus is coming.

The second set of four Beatitudes are blessings for those disciples actively working for the coming exodus, laboring for the coming of God's kingdom—those filled with mercy and who work with purity of heart to make *shalom*/peace,[25] and who stand up for righteousness/justice for the poor. The last of the eight Beatitudes is repeated as the ninth Beatitude, the persecuted will be rewarded. The Beatitudes are stunningly insightful as an analysis of oppression, and also an exodus-road to the promised land of the kingdom of heaven on earth.

The promise of "for theirs is the kingdom of heaven" ends the first and eighth Beatitude. Righteousness/justice is used in the fourth and the eighth Beatitude.[26] Again the Beatitudes are crafted with beautiful literary precision.

A psychological reflection on the Beatitudes includes the following ideas. Pain and suffering are a very real part of human life, and unavoidable. People can get stuck in unhelpful ways of responding to pain and suffering. In Acceptance and Commitment Therapy (ACT),[27] a person works towards finding new ways to respond to their pain and suffering, allowing them to move forward in life in ways that are value-driven, give meaning, are justice-making, and create authentic community. The idea that the

---

23. Mark A. Powell, cited in Blomberg, "Most Often Abused Verses," 4–5. Bredin, *Jesus, Revolutionary of the Poor*, 142. Yang, "Sermon on the Mount/Plain," 846.

24. Bredin, *Jesus, Revolutionary of the Poor*, 126.

25. *Shalom* is the Hebrew word for a holistic peace that includes material well-being and prosperity, justice, integrity/honesty, and straightforwardness. The Greek translation in the New Testament is *eirene* and includes reconciliation. *Shalom* and *eirene* are fuller, stronger words than the English word *peace*. See Yoder, *Shalom*, 10–23.

26. Bredin, *Jesus, Revolutionary of the Poor*, 142. Yang, "Sermon on the Mount/Plain," 846–847.

27. "Psychological Inflexibility."

Beatitudes are steps suggests one can begin with small wins that then build momentum. A journey of a thousand miles begins with one step. The poor in spirit, the poorest of the poor, are promised the kingdom of heaven. The kingdom of God comes a little closer by taking the first step of hope.[28]

THE LADDER OF THE BEATITUDES

We can also explore how the Beatitudes are concrete steps of blessing on the path into the new reality of the kingdom of God. As the Twelve Steps of Alcoholics Anonymous describe action steps to stop drinking and live a life of sobriety, so one reading of the Beatitudes is to see them as eight steps into kingdom life.

Jim Forest left the US Navy after becoming a Catholic and conscientious objector. He served for a time in a Catholic Worker community, and was also an activist against the Vietnam war, working with the Fellowship of Reconciliation. He later joined the Orthodox Church. Forest suggests the idea of a ladder to understand how the Beatitudes work:

> The eight beatitudes are all aspects of being in communion with God. They are like rungs on a ladder. Each one leads to the next. Remove any one of them, and you fall off the ladder. It is a carefully built ladder. The rungs aren't in a random order. To reach the second step, we need to make the first step.[29]

THE BEATITUDES—A GRACE JOURNEY

From poverty of spirit to standing up for justice, the ladder of the Beatitudes looks difficult, daunting, hard. Is it possible for ordinary humans to climb each Beatitude step? It is true that the first disciples, like us, often fall off the ladder. However, later in Matthew, Jesus promises us that faith the size of a tiny mustard seed can grow and move mountains.[30] Each Beatitude is an expression of love. God's love releases the power to love in us, and enables us to grow in love through the steps of the Beatitudes. We do not travel alone; we have the help of fellow disciples. At the end of Matthew's

---

28. Author's conversation with Dr. James Rathbone, consultant clinical psychologist.

29. Forest, "Climb the Ladder of the Beatitudes," 25. See also Forest, *Ladder of the Beatitudes*.

30. Matthew 17:20.

Gospel, Jesus promises to be with us always.[31] The Holy Spirit helps us, and Paul writes about how the fruits of the Holy Spirit can grow in our lives.[32] The Beatitudes are a grace trail, a path along which we are empowered by the Holy Spirit as we exercise faith. We also do not walk alone. There is the grace of others encouraging and helping us. The Beatitudes are not a solo climb, but a communal journey, taken together, and we should leave no one behind.

To use Paul's language, the journey of a disciple has two stages. The first is called justification. This is first discovering grace, that God loves us no matter what we have done. The second stage is called sanctification. This is growing in grace, the transformation of our character to be more and more like Jesus. The first Beatitude, "Blessed are the poor in spirit," corresponds to justification—grace for the poor in spirit. By grace we are promised the kingdom of heaven. The next seven Beatitudes describe the process of sanctification, the transformation of our lives into faithful disciples of Jesus.

Both teachings of justification and sanctification are found in other New Testament texts, particularly in the writings of Paul.[33] They are two aspects of salvation. First justification—discovering we are loved, that we are forgiven, pardoned no matter what we have done. Faith is believing, trusting, and accepting this gift. This begins our journey. Second, we are to be remade, transformed. Sanctification is the work of God's love in us to make us loving. Justification is the gift of God of God's grace. Sanctification is the ongoing work of grace that is transforming us, and enables us to endure the ups and downs of growing, learning, and changing. Faith is trusting God will not let us go.

Where does the ladder take us, where do the Beatitudes lead us? It is important to understand that the Beatitudes have a destination. Jesus' disciples are to become salt, light, a city on a hill. We will explore in the next chapter the implications and challenge of Matthew 5:13–16.

The rest of the Sermon on the Mount is in some ways a commentary on the Beatitudes.

---

31. Matthew 28:20.
32. Galatians 5:22–23.
33. Justification references include Romans 3:23, 5:1–2. Sanctification references include Romans 5:1–5, Romans 12:1–2, 2 Corinthians 5:17, and Galatians 5:22–26.

REFLECTIONS

1. What blessings for you do you see in the Beatitudes?
2. How do the Beatitudes express grace, good news, for those living in difficult times?
3. What hope can be found in each Beatitude? What is the hope when all the Beatitudes are taken together?
4. What do you think of the Beatitudes as a ladder taking us on eight steps of discipleship, a path of discipleship? How would climbing the steps of the Beatitudes transform your life? How is grace a part of the journey?
5. Reread each Beatitude and think how each one is exemplified in the life and story of Jesus. What is the importance of Jesus demonstrating each Beatitude in his life?
6. Could you write a new Beatitude? Share it with others if you are doing this as a group study.

Prayer Thought

Loving God, help me accept and practice the gift of each Beatitude. Help me see each Beatitude in your son Jesus so I can better follow as a disciple. Amen.

4

Salt, Light, a City on a Hill

INTRODUCTION

As a young adult, after a somewhat traumatic childhood, I was looking for a better world. I did not have biblical ideas of the kingdom of God on earth, but that is what I was looking for. I had a yearning, a sense of direction, and a trust that God could help. With a degree in horticulture and later working on a PhD in plant genetics, I hoped to make a contribution to feeding the world. Working in Germany for a year between degrees was part of this journey, and I discovered a loving church congregation near Hannover with many young adults interested in peace and justice. They were like a city on a hill and they were very loving to me, despite my being British. A year later, now in South Wales, I was baptized in this denomination. I felt the call of the kingdom, I wanted to be part of a movement that wanted to be "cities on hills."

Later, my wife, Jewell, and I lived for a year with our two sons in the Bruderhof, an intentional Christian community, holding all things in common in East Sussex, England. Later, for twenty years, we lived in another intentional Christian community in Independence, Missouri. So, I come to this passage in the Sermon on the Mount knowing firsthand that there are indeed exemplary Christian communities, inspiring, yet very human. I also remember that the early Jerusalem Christians formed the first such community described in Acts 2 and Acts 4:32–35. They were an Exodus community of right relationships, full of Spirit, hope, and sharing.

Part Two | Sermon on the Mount

First Thoughts

Read the following passage:

> 5:13 "You are the salt of the earth; but if salt has lost its taste, how can its saltiness be restored? It is no longer good for anything, but is thrown out and trampled under foot.
> 14 "You are the light of the world. A city built on a hill cannot be hid. 15 No one after lighting a lamp puts it under the bushel basket, but on the lampstand, and it gives light to all in the house. 16 In the same way, let your light shine before others, so that they may see your good works and give glory to your Father in heaven. (Matthew 5:13–16)

1. What is the message of this passage? Can you put it into your own words?

2. How might this passage connect with the Beatitudes that come just before it?

UNDERSTANDING SALT, LIGHT, A CITY ON A HILL

The Beatitudes equip us to be witnesses together, in practical ways of living God's kingdom. We are to become salt, light, a city on a hill. In this passage, notice how Jesus has switched here to saying *you*.[1] He began this switch in Matthew 5:11–12 with the last Beatitude, about persecution. He is saying to

---

1. Du Toit, "Revisiting the Sermon on the Mount," 75.

the first disciples, don't worry when you are persecuted, rejoice and be glad, *you* are the salt of the earth, the light of the world, a city on a hill. Matthew also has Jesus saying *you* to the first congregation that heard this gospel, perhaps in Antioch. But Jesus is also saying *you* to us, 2,000 years later. Jesus is personally encouraging all of us directly whether we are disciples of yesteryear or today.

We have a destination. A people shaped by the Beatitudes are to be a "signal community" of hope, a foretaste of the kingdom. It is not yet the transformation of the whole world, but it is a beginning.

Caesar's Roman Empire came by marching soldiers in legions bringing death, destruction, crucifixion, and extractive taxation. God's kingdom comes by salty challenge and witness together. The Beatitudes lead to witness and invitation, to just, merciful relationships, not domination.

"You are the salt of the earth . . ."

A little salt seasons the whole pot. Salt, sodium chloride, is also a preservative in a hot climate with no refrigerators. There is also another kind of salt possibly implied here. I learned as a boy from my farming parents that when wood is burned, the remaining wood ash is rich in potassium chloride, and other potassium salts. This is an excellent fertilizer. However, my parents would warn me that if it rains on wood ash, the potassium salts are leached out, and the wood ash is no longer any good as a fertilizer and is just thrown away. Farmers 2,000 years ago would have almost certainly known this—ashes thrown out from spent fires would cause better plant growth where they landed. Slash-and-burn cultivators understand well the increased fertility of land cleared by burning. If disciples are not shaped by Jesus' teachings they are ineffective—they cannot season, preserve, or help others grow.

Salt is small, hidden, and yet has a powerful effect. Later in Matthew's Gospel, Jesus talks about the kingdom of heaven in two parables, about a mustard seed and yeast ("leaven" in King James Bible English). Jesus says the mustard seed is the smallest of seeds, but has the capacity to become a tree. Likewise, Jesus talks how a little yeast can grow in bread dough until all the dough rises.[2] Salt, mustard seed, and yeast are metaphors for the power of small groups of faithful disciples to bless and transform their societies.

---

2. Matthew 13:31–33.

Part Two | Sermon on the Mount

"You are the light of the world. A city built on a hill cannot be hid."

A lighthouse, a small point of light, guides ships safely in dangerous waters. The city of Jerusalem is a city on a hill, nearly 2,500 feet, or 800 meters above sea level. Lights from fires and lamps in the city would be seen for miles around. The name *Jerusalem* means city of peace, yet it has been destroyed at least twice, besieged twenty-three times, captured and recaptured forty-four times, and attacked fifty-two times.[3] Nevertheless, the *new* Jerusalem will be a city of peace. Its citizens will be a forgiven, meek people, living justly together, practicing mercy with one another and forgiving others, pure in heart, and peacemakers. Then the visions of the prophet Isaiah shall be fulfilled. Followers of the Prince of Peace will be a true temple people. Their swords will be beaten into plowshares, lion and lamb will lie down together, a little child shall lead them, and violence will be ended.[4] On that day the followers of Jesus, the Messiah King, shaped by the Beatitudes, shall point to him and "shall stand as a signal to the peoples; the nations shall inquire of him, and his dwelling shall be glorious."[5]

A small but Jesus-shaped group of people can influence the whole world, beginning with one community. The later parables of mustard seed and leaven/yeast reinforce the possibility of dynamic change from small, insignificant beginnings.[6] A people who live the Beatitudes change the world together, step by step:

Salt, Light, City on a Hill[7]

Blessed are those persecuted for justice sake
Blessed are the peacemakers
Blessed are the pure in heart
Blessed are the merciful
Blessed are those who hunger and thirst for justice
Blessed are the meek
Blessed are those who mourn
Blessed are the poor in spirit

---

3. Eric H. Cline, cited in Katz, "Do We Divide the Holiest Holy City?," 1.
4. Isaiah 9:6; 2:2–4; 11:6–9.
5. Isaiah 11:10.
6. Matthew 13:31–33.
7. Matthew 5:3–12, adapted.

Salt, Light, a City on a Hill

Disciples, on a journey of conversion through God's grace, can participate in new social ways of righteous living. The kingdom of God comes through personal and systemic change. New social systems without new, transformed people end in failure. The bright hopes of a better world can be disappointed by not effectively addressing personal change. New people in new systems, overcoming sin in both, is what Jesus is teaching here. The Beatitudes are about creating a new people to be the new Jerusalem, not from a spiritual elite, but from the broken and the humble. Matthew 5:1–12 could be summarized by the headline, "Remade people remake a new world." New wine in new wineskins, said Jesus.[8] Grace enables both.

How did the early Christians actually live as disciples?

Early church scholar Alan Kreider describes the rigorous discipleship process used to make new Christians in the first 300 years. Sometimes Christian apprenticeship lasted longer than three years. It was a thorough process that involved resocialization from pagan values and habits to Christ's way. What was the result, how were early Christians salt, light, and a city on a hill? They fed their own poor and the poor of their neighbors, they cared for children without parents, they looked after old slaves and prisoners. They buried the dead, no matter how poor, with dignity. In times of plague they nursed the sick, whether Christian or pagan. Outsiders said, "*Vide*, look! How they love one another."[9] There was no other missionary strategy, just being together as salt, light, a city on a hill. As Christian teacher Lactantius said, "We teach, we show, we demonstrate."[10]

CITIES ON HILLS AND PROPHETIC IMAGINATION

Christians are to live the teachings of Jesus, including the Sermon on the Mount, together. They are to be signal communities, contrast communities, which demonstrate the presence of the kingdom of God in their nonviolence, economic sharing, care for each other, and in care for others. They do this in their life together. The kingdom of God comes by being salt, light, a demonstration community.

The first subversive, repentant act in any society is imagining a better one. Old Testament scholar Walter Brueggemann speaks of prophetic

---

8. Matthew 9:17.
9. Kreider, *Patient Ferment*, 61–65.
10. Kreider, *Patient Ferment*, 259, 275–76.

imagination.[11] I want to suggest that imagination of a just world, a city on a hill, is the first prophetic action. The kingdom of God has first to be imagined before it can be.

REFLECTIONS

1. The kingdom of God comes through personal and systemic change. What system changes are needed in our world? What personal changes are required of me? How do the Beatitudes help me be part of salt, light, city on a hill?

2. Read the parables of the mustard seed and yeast/leaven told later in Matthew's Gospel (Matthew 13:31–33). Are salt, light, mustard seed, and yeast good metaphors for the effectiveness of grassroot communities of disciples living out the Sermon on the Mount? To what extent is this a believable and effective strategy of change?

3. What would it mean to practice prophetic imagination in our neighborhood?

4. To what extent is your congregation already a city on a hill? What would it mean to go further?

5. Are there really two very different destinations possible in our world—mass murder, war, hunger, and climate apocalypse, or green cities of justice and mercy on metaphorical hills? Does thinking about these two options help clarify your decision about really following Jesus?

Prayer Thought

God beyond imagination, help me imagine a better world and follow your way. Give me courage to be salt, light, part of a city on a hill. Help me see your kingdom on earth as it is in heaven. May this possibility be bright in my soul. Give me ears to hear your call and the strength to live it with others. Amen.

---

11. Brueggemann, *Prophetic Imagination*.

5

Jesus Affirms the Law and the Prophets

INTRODUCTION

Read the passage:

> 5 [17] "Do not think that I have come to abolish the law or the prophets; I have come not to abolish but to fulfill. [18] For truly I tell you, until heaven and earth pass away, not one letter, not one stroke of a letter, will pass from the law until all is accomplished. [19] Therefore, whoever breaks one of the least of these commandments, and teaches others to do the same, will be called least in the kingdom of heaven; but whoever does them and teaches them will be called great in the kingdom of heaven. [20] For I tell you, unless your righteousness exceeds that of the scribes and Pharisees, you will never enter the kingdom of heaven.
> (Matthew 5:17–20)

First Thoughts

1. What do you think Jesus is saying here?

2. If you were to summarize the message of the Jewish Law and the Prophets in about three sentences, what might you say?

LAW, PROPHETS, AND JAMES YEN

Why does Jesus begin by affirming the Jewish Law and the Prophets?

Some years ago, I did a course at the International Institute of Rural Reconstruction (IIRR) in Cavite, Philippines. Here I learned about James Yen, the founder of IIRR, who had been involved in mass education in China, and later in rural development programs of health, education, environment, and livelihood in many countries for millions of people.[1] He famously said this:

> Go to the people
> Live among them
> Learn from them
> Love them
> Serve them
> Plan with them
> Start with what they know
> Build on what they have.[2]

In some ways this describes Jesus' strategy for creating a movement for the transformation of first Israel, and then the whole world. It ends with these words,

> Start with what they know
> Build on what they have.

By emphasizing the Torah and the Prophets, Jesus was starting with what the people knew, and building on what they had. Yen called himself a

---

1. Wikipedia, "Institute of Rural Reconstruction."
2. Yen, AZQuotes.

follower of Jesus Christ, but was critical of missionaries who did not concern themselves with life and needs in the rural villages.[3]

As humans we can be resistant to change. The poor are understandably conservative psychologically. Survival when you are already vulnerable may depend on taking minimal risks. Starting with what people know is affirming of their dignity and their culture, that they have something to build on. To remind Israelite peasants of the story of Exodus, that the Torah and the Prophets speak of a God who is on the side of slaves, the poor, the stranger, the widow, and the fatherless, is empowering.[4]

Jesus stands in the tradition of the Torah Law and the Prophets. What did this mean for the first disciples? What does it mean for us today?

TORAH LAW AND THE TWO GREATEST COMMANDMENTS

> "Do not think that I have come to abolish the law or the prophets;
> I have come not to abolish but to fulfill." (Matthew 5:17)

In this passage Jesus affirms the faith of Israel. Let us begin with the centrality of the Torah (Genesis, Exodus, Leviticus, Numbers, and Deuteronomy) as revelation for God's people.

Matthew is writing his Gospel for Jewish Christians before the two faiths have separated. Matthew's Jesus highly values Jewish Scripture. He is also beginning with what the people know, and building on what they have in order to help them understand and participate in the good news of the kingdom of heaven in a time of Roman oppression.

But how does Jesus read the Torah? There is a lot of detail. In the Talmud of later Judaism, 613 commandments are said to be found in the Torah.[5] This of course includes the Ten Commandments, which Jesus quotes and affirms.[6] Are all these 613 commandments equally important? Matthew later in the Gospel gives an answer.

---

3. Wikipedia, "Y. C. James Yen."
4. Author conversation with James Rathbone.
5. Hecht, "613 Commandments."
6. For instance, Jesus tells the rich young man that to have eternal life, he should keep the commandments, and illustrates with examples from the Ten Commandments. See Matthew 19:18–19.

When asked by a Jewish lawyer, "Which is the greatest commandment?' Matthew's Jesus said this:

> "'You shall love the Lord your God with all your heart, and with all your soul, and with all your mind.' This is the greatest and first commandment. And a second is like it: 'You shall love your neighbor as yourself.' On these two commandments hang all the law and the prophets."[7]

These two commandments thus simply summarize all the commandments and state their intent—to love God and love our neighbor as ourselves. Yet how is the second commandment like the first? All humans are created in the image of God![8] So to love your neighbor as yourself is also to love God. "On these two commandments hang all the law and the prophets," said Jesus.[9]

"You shall love the Lord your God with all your heart, and with all your soul, and with all your might"[10] is a summary of the first three of the Ten Commandments. "You shall love your neighbor as yourself" (Leviticus 19:18) is a summary of the last seven of the Ten Commandments.

Indeed, famous Jewish sages also used "love your neighbor as yourself" as a summary. For instance, Rabbi Akiva, a second-century-CE sage, said: "Love your neighbor as yourself. This is a great general principle in the Torah."[11]

THE PROPHETS

In the time of Jesus, the Hebrew Bible included the major prophets Isaiah, Jeremiah, and Ezekiel, and the minor prophets, "The Twelve," including Hosea, Amos, Micah, Zechariah, and Malachi.

Moses is claimed as the greatest of the prophets. By tradition he is the inspired author of the Torah, both written and oral. The burning bush story begins with Moses being called by name. Moses is the first in a tradition of prophetic voices for the poor.

---

7. Matthew 22:37–40.
8. Genesis 1:26–27.
9. Matthew 22:40.
10. Deuteronomy 6:4–5.
11. Collins, "Love Your Neighbor."

Jesus Affirms the Law and the Prophets

Abraham J. Heschel, a Polish-American Jewish scholar who escaped the Holocaust, wrote a book called simply *The Prophets*. In his first chapter he writes what it means to be a prophet:

> [The prophet] is thrown into orations about widows and orphans, about the corruption of judges and affairs of the market place. Instead of showing a way through the elegant mansions of the mind, the prophets take us to the slums . . .[12]
>
> Prophecy is the voice that God has lent to the silent agony, a voice to the plundered poor, to the profaned riches of the world . . . God is raging in the prophet's words . . .[13] [The prophet's] images must not shine, they must burn . . .[14] The prophet's word is a scream in the night. While the world is at ease and asleep, the prophet feels the blast from heaven.[15]

Heschel (1907–1972) was himself something of a prophet. He marched with Martin Luther King Jr. in the civil rights movement, and spoke against the Vietnam War.

Amos, Micah, and Isaiah are some of my favorite prophets. The message of the prophets can be summarized as follows, "Thus says the Lord of hosts: Render true judgements, show kindness and mercy to one another; do not oppress the widow, the orphan, the alien, or the poor; and do not devise evil in your hearts against one another."[16]

> Not one letter, not one stroke of a letter, will pass from the law until all is accomplished. (Matthew 5:18)

The Hebrew Bible is written in a kind of shorthand, without vowels. This sometimes gives the possibility of many interpretations, depending on what vowels are thought to make the most sense. So, there is discussion and debate about the right reading. There is no pope in Judaism to settle things. The rabbis and the community must work on what is really meant together.

> Unless your righteousness exceeds that of the scribes and Pharisees, you will never enter the kingdom of heaven. (Matthew 5:20)

---

12. Heschel, *Prophets*, 3.
13. Heschel, *Prophets*, 5–6.
14. Heschel, *Prophets*, 8.
15. Heschel, *Prophets*, 19.
16. Zechariah 7:10.

Walter Brueggemann argues that the tradition of Sinai and exodus are the authentic tradition of the Torah and the Prophets. To love your neighbor as yourself is to live for the common good. Brueggemann argues that from Kings David and Solomon down to King Herod the tradition of exploitive Pharaoh returned, cloaked in a faked religion of Israel, and centered in a temple system that exploited the poor. Brueggemann points us to stories of prophetic resistance to the kings of Israel who were being Pharaohs all over again.[17] The disciples of Jesus are called to a greater righteousness than that of the scribes and Pharisees, the priests, and the monarchy.

We live in a time of political populism and neoliberal economics, continuing racism and patriarchy, in which the prophetic tradition of compassion for the stranger, the widow and the fatherless is urgently relevant and challengingly needed. According to Jesus in his movement, beginning with the Sermon on the Mount, not one letter, not one stroke of a letter will pass away from the liberating story of exodus and the burning words of the Prophets until the new Jerusalem, the kingdom of heaven, cities on hills, shall fully come.

REFLECTIONS

1. Jesus is a rabbi and values his Jewish Scriptures, and like all rabbis was teaching and interpreting them. What are some of your favorite Old Testament Scriptures?

2. What does it mean to speak up for and stand with the widow, the orphan, and the stranger today? What are some of the Gospel stories that speak up for the marginalized?

3. Did the kings of Israel become new Pharaohs? Are the prophets of Israel following Moses' resistance to exploitive power? Who are Pharaohs today? Who are today's prophets resisting them? Where are we as disciples called to be?

4. Jewish philosopher Michael Walzer has suggested that "the exodus narrative is the taproot of all revolutions in the modern world."[18] What do you think?

---

17. Brueggemann, *Journey to the Common Good*. See also Brueggemann, "Jesus Acted Out the Alternative to Empire."

18. Cited in Brueggemann, *Journey to the Common Good*, 43.

Jesus Affirms the Law and the Prophets

Prayer Thought

Thank you, God, for your love, that seeks to reclaim us individually and collectively from our lostness and injustice. In your love we have an ever fresh and new beginning. Let me awaken in my soul an openness to your love. May your love release the power to love in me so justice and shalom peace may come on earth as it is in heaven. Help me also stand up for the poor and vulnerable. Amen.

6

Six Discipleship Commandments

INTRODUCTION

Jesus next teaches six discipleship commandments. Read the following extracts from Matthew 5:21–48:

> "You have heard that it was said to those of ancient times, 'You shall not murder'; and 'whoever murders shall be liable to judgment.' But I say to you that if you are angry with a brother or sister, you will be liable to judgment . . ."—Matthew 5:21–22
>
> "You have heard that it was said, 'You shall not commit adultery.' But I say to you that everyone who looks at a woman with lust has already committed adultery with her in his heart."—Matthew 5:27–28
>
> "It was also said, 'Whoever divorces his wife, let him give her a certificate of divorce.' But I say to you that anyone who divorces his wife, except on the ground of unchastity, causes her to commit adultery; and whoever marries a divorced woman commits adultery." —Matthew 5:31–32
>
> "Again, you have heard that it was said to those of ancient times, 'You shall not swear falsely, but carry out the vows you have made to the Lord.' But I say to you, Do not swear at all . . ."—Matthew 5:33–34
>
> "You have heard that it was said, 'An eye for an eye and tooth for a tooth.' But I say to you, Do not resist an evildoer . . ."—Matthew 5:38–39

Six Discipleship Commandments

"You have heard that it was said, 'You shall love your neighbour and hate your enemy.' But I say to you, Love your enemies and pray for those who persecute you . . ."—Matthew 5:43–44

FIRST THOUGHTS

1. What patterns do you see in these extracts?

2. Is Jesus contradicting, correcting, or deepening each Torah commandment quoted?

CONTRADICTING, CORRECTING, OR DEEPENING THE TORAH?

We are now going to look at these six discipleship commandments dealing with murder, adultery, divorce, oaths, retaliation, and enemies. Why these six topics and in this order? Life is important and "Thou shalt not murder" is one of the Ten Commandments. "Thou shalt not commit adultery" is the next of the Ten Commandments, and lust can lead to adultery. Adultery seriously disrupts family, has great consequences in village life, and can also lead to murder. Next is divorce, the painful division of a couple and family, and this can again be connected with adultery. So, the first three discipleship commandments are derived from two important commandments in the Ten Commandments—"Do not murder" and "Do not commit adultery."[1]

1. Deuteronomy 5:17–18.

What about the next three commandments—oaths, retaliation, and enemies? These three commandments can be found in Leviticus 19:12, 17, and 18. Truth-telling/not swearing oaths is foundational to trust, and contributes to healthy, peaceful community. This commandment is in Leviticus 19:12, and is also connected to two of the Ten Commandments: "Thou shalt not take God's name in vain" and "Thou shalt not bear false witness."[2] Non-retaliation (not taking revenge), and "Love your neighbor as yourself" only applies to fellow Israelites in this Leviticus passage. However, Matthew's Jesus has made it apply to everyone.[3] Jesus goes further and intensifies and universalizes these last two commandments. Is Jesus contradicting the Torah commandment, or fulfilling its original intent?

In Matthew 5:21–48 we encounter the following formula, six times for each of these discipleship commandments: "You have heard that it was said ... But I say to you ..." The first statement is called a thesis and the second statement an antithesis, or contradiction:

> You have heard that it was said ... [thesis statement]
> But I say to you ... [antithesis or contradictory response]

This formula was a common rabbinic practice in Jesus' day. Jewish scholar Pinchas Lapide argues that the formula should be understood not as thesis/antithesis, but as thesis/superthesis: "Jesus furnishes us ... not with antitheses but with 'supertheses,' which deepen, intensify, and radicalize the biblical commandments—guiding us back to their roots and original intention."[4]

The idea of thesis and antithesis can be helpful for us to hear Jesus' challenging and confronting messages that we hear from our cultures today. Lapide's argument that Jesus is giving us supertheses rather than antitheses also helps remind us that Jesus is not seeking to contradict the Jewish Law or Torah, but rather to intensify it, stand within it, and bring into clear focus its commitment to life.

Certainly, dealing with anger and lust to prevent murder and adultery is intensification of the Law. Jesus is getting to the root cause (anger and lust), not just the results (murder and adultery). However, for the next four—divorce, oaths, retaliation, and love of enemies—Jesus also appears

---

2. Deuteronomy 5:11, 20.

3. Goldstone, "Structure of Matthew's Antitheses." Goldstone in addition to exploring Scripture goes into rabbinic and also Christian ways of dealing with these passages from the Ten Commandments and Leviticus 19:12, 17–18.

4. Lapide, *Sermon on the Mount*, 46.

Six Discipleship Commandments

to be significantly changing the law. How can Jesus claim to be conservative about Scripture in Matthew 5:17–20, and then be changing specifics of the Law?

Scholars explore different ways of how this might be done. One way is to argue that Jesus is challenging the oral law traditions of the Scribes and Pharisees, and restating the original intention given to Moses on Sinai. Another is that Jesus is correcting how other Jewish groups, for example the Essene community living in Qumran, are stating these commandments.[5]

Dale Allison states that Jesus' teachings "surpass those of the Torah, without contradicting the Torah" and that Jesus is examining intention as well as the external act.[6] Allison thus agrees with Lapide that Jesus is deepening, intensifying, and radicalizing the biblical commandments, but is not overturning the law.[7]

One can also argue theologically that it is actually Jesus that originally gave the law to Moses on Sinai, and he thus has unique authority to correct the misunderstandings of both Moses and those teachers after Moses. Matthew near the beginning of his Gospel states, "and they shall name him Emmanuel, which means, 'God is with us.'"[8] Is the One on the Mount, before the crowds and the disciples, greater than Moses, and is he the One who actually spoke to Moses? Matthew writes at the end of the Sermon on the Mount: "Now when Jesus had finished saying these things, the crowds were astounded at his teaching, for he taught them as one having authority, and not as their scribes."[9]

TWO PARTS OR THREE PARTS—DYADS OR TRIADS?

So far, we have seen just two parts to each of the six discipleship statements in Matthew 5:21–48. Here it is again:

1. You have heard that it was said . . . [thesis statement]
2. But I say to you . . . [antithesis or contradictory response]

---

5. See Marcus, "Enigmas of the Antitheses," 121–37, for a fuller discussion.
6. Allison Jr., *Sermon on the Mount*, 33.
7. Allison Jr., *Sermon on the Mount*, 31.
8. Matthew 1:23.
9. Matthew 7:28–29.

These two parts are called a *dyad* or pair. Glen Stassen, however, sees not just two parts, but three parts (*triad*) to each discipleship commandment. Scholars have often tended to miss seeing a possible third part. Stassen's three parts making up a triad are as follows:

1. *Traditional righteousness.* This is a commandment in the Torah. For example, one of the Ten Commandments, "You shall not murder . . ."
2. *Vicious cycle plus judgment.* If you get angry, insult, or call someone a fool, you will suffer judgement. It makes the conflict worse and becomes a vicious cycle.
3. *Transforming Initiative.* These are actions you can take to end the conflict and bring reconciliation. For example, before you worship, reconcile with a brother or sister; when on your way to court, come to a settlement before you debate in court.[10]

Seeing this triad structure opens up a deeper way of understanding each of these six discipleship commandments. Stassen goes on to say that there are fourteen triads in Matthew 5:21–7:12. He counts a total of seventy-five triads and very few dyads in the whole of Matthew's Gospel.[11] Davies and Allison also point out how Matthew is packed full of triads. Matthew thinks and writes often in threes.[12] Doing things is threes is a teaching device that makes it easier to remember important points.

I find Stassen's three parts (traditional righteousness, vicious cycle, and transforming initiative) insightful in throwing new light on Jesus' teachings of the six discipleship commandments described in Matthew 5:21–48.

For each discipleship commandment, the emphasis now changes from the second part to the third part. For murder, the focus changes from not getting angry to the transforming initiative, reconciling as soon as you can. We can find a way to escape the vicious cycle described in the second part. It changes from an almost impossible high ideal to a grace-based practical action. This is still challenging and requires courage, but is possible.[13]

Using Stassen's three parts we will look in more detail at the first discipleship commandment—reconcile.

---

10. Stassen, "Fourteen Triads," 267.
11. Stassen, "Fourteen Triads," 268.
12. Davies and Allison Jr., *Matthew 1–7*, 62–64.
13. Stassen, "Fourteen Triads," 268–69.

REFLECTIONS

1. There are six discipleship commandments, on murder, lust, divorce, not swearing oaths/truth-telling, non-retaliation, and loving enemies. What are your first, honest responses to these? To what extent do you see these six discipleship commandments are really about loving our neighbor as ourselves?

2. These discipleship commandments are connected to several of the Ten Commandments in Deuteronomy 5:6–21. Why is it important for Jesus to go back to the Ten Commandments?

3. Look through Matthew 5:21–48 and find this reoccurring structure:

    a. You have heard that it was said . . . [thesis statement]

    b. But I say to you . . . [antithesis or contradictory response]
    How does Jesus' "But I say to you . . ." change things?

4. Glen Stassen sees three-part structures (triads) rather than two-part structures (dyads). How might this three-part structure be helpful for a better understanding of these six discipleship commandments?

Prayer Thought

Loving God, these six discipleship commandments are a big challenge. I cannot keep these commandments using only my own strength. With your grace, love, and the help of brothers and sisters, help me be diligent in living them. Amen.

7

Discipleship Commandment 1: Reconcile!

The Traditional Righteousness	The Vicious Cycle plus judgement	The Transforming Initiative
is presented as coming from the Jewish tradition. It occurs first in a three-part structure.	is presented as Jesus' teaching. It diagnoses an issue and shows how it leads to ongoing problems and judgement.	is also presented as Jesus' teaching. Its main verb is a positive "must do"—an initiative, not a negative "must not." It calls for doing something to escape from the vicious cycle and to participate in the reign of God/God's kingdom.[1]

---

1. For these headings and descriptions, I have adapted Stassen, "Fourteen Triads," Table 1.

Discipleship Commandment 1: Reconcile!

Matthew 5:21—"You have heard that it was said to those of ancient times, 'You shall not murder'; and 'whoever murders shall be liable to judgement.'"	[22] But I say to you that if you are angry with a brother or sister, you will be liable to judgement; and if you insult a brother or sister, you will be liable to the council; and if you say, "You fool," you will be liable to the hell of fire.	[23] So when you are offering your gift at the altar, if you remember that your brother or sister has something against you, [24] leave your gift there before the altar and go; first be reconciled to your brother or sister, and then come and offer your gift. [25] Come to terms quickly with your accuser while you are on the way to court with him, or your accuser may hand you over to the judge, and the judge to the guard, and you will be thrown into prison. [26] Truly I tell you, you will never get out until you have paid the last penny.

"You shall not murder" is one of the Ten Commandments.[2] Jesus first says anger is dangerous, and insulting a brother or sister is really bad. Anger and insults increase the emotions in a conflict. It can take us spinning into a vicious cycle that makes a situation worse. Anger can push us over the cliff edge into violence and actual murder.

The Jewish Talmud makes the connection between shaming and killing very clear: "A teacher of Mishna taught before Rav Nahman, son of Isaac: 'If anyone makes the face of a companion pale before a crowd, it is as if he shed blood.' He said to him: 'That is excellently stated.'"[3] So, to call a person a fool is deeply shaming. It is also deeply shaming to insult someone because of their gender, orientation, race, national origin, religion, weight, height, and so on.

Yet conflict in the fellowship of the church, or at work, or in the neighborhood, or in the home, is unavoidable. We are all human. Anger turned inward can lead to depression and self-harm. Anger turned outward can lead to murder. What are some healthy ways of dealing with anger in the congregation or elsewhere? My mother told my brothers and I to count to

---

2. Exodus 20:13 and Deuteronomy 5:17.
3. Lapide, *Sermon on the Mount*, 50.

ten. That gives time for our brains to switch from fight or flight to reasoning, from the reptilian, instinctive part of our brains, to the thinking part of our brains.

Later, in chapter 18 of Matthew's Gospel, Jesus teaches a practical way to deal with conflict:

Step 1	If someone upsets you, speak to them directly and alone. If you can sort out the issue then the problem is solved. Nobody else need know about your conflict. The fellowship is healed.
Step 2	If you cannot solve the issue together ask someone you both trust to help mediate. Both steps 1 and 2 prevent gossip behind people's backs, which poisons Christian fellowship and injures community.
Step 3	If mediation does not solve the problem, then the conflict is brought into the open, and the leaders, and even the whole congregation, attempt to solve it.[4]

Jesus promises that when two or three are together and trying to resolve a conflict, he is present with them.[5] Finally, Jesus teaches about the importance of forgiving one another.[6] Without forgiveness, conflicts cannot be resolved. Learning to solve conflicts with brothers and sisters is an apprenticeship in learning peacemaking skills, which we can apply to making peace in the world.

How do we deal with our anger? It helps to understand our human brains. Very simply we have the animal part of our brain, instinctive, wired for survival—fight or flight. Then there is the frontal cortex of the brain that is able to do clever things; it is the thinking, human, problem-solving, rational part of our brain. When my mother said count to ten before acting on my anger, that is a strategy to switch from our animal brain to our rational human brain. Murder can be the fruit of anger. Understanding anger and having strategies to reconcile are effective psychological interventions that can prevent murder. Angry? Count to ten, or say the Lord's Prayer. Then use the thinking part of your brain to problem-solve creatively.[7]

Act by doing a transformative initiative—reconcile quickly. And if that is not possible, bring in a mediator, or even the grace of the whole church to solve the conflict, as described in Matthew 18:15–35.

---

4. Matthew 18:15–35.

5. Matthew 18:20. We often think this passage is encouragement for small prayer meetings, but actually the context is conflict resolution.

6. Matthew 18:21–35.

7. Author conversation with James Rathbone.

Discipleship Commandment 1: Reconcile!

If the sayings that make up the Sermon on the Mount were first written down in Galilee, this is about someone from Galilee offering a sacrifice at the Jerusalem temple. Walking one way between Galilee and Jerusalem took several days. Imagine getting to the Jerusalem temple, and being ready to sacrifice, but then remembering that someone in your village has a grudge against you. Jesus is saying you have to leave the sacrificial animal and go back home to reconcile first. Only then will your sacrifice on the altar mean something. Offering a sacrifice at the temple was about forgiveness, making atonement, reconciliation with God. To do this with integrity means being at peace with others.

Reconcile! Make peace with others! Then come to worship God! Reconciliation is the heart of true worship. Make peace with others before communion, then take communion. This was an important discipline practiced very seriously in the early church for the first 300 years. It was inspired by this passage.[8]

Christian disciples sort out issues without going to the courts, which in Jesus' day were biased towards the rich anyway. Use someone you both trust in the fellowship of the congregation to help mediate. There is an urgency to reconciliation.

REFLECTIONS

1. How can I use the energy of anger to confront an issue without harming the relationship long-term? Is making sure things are cleared up before communion or worship a good practice?

2. Have you been insulted verbally or called a name? What did that feel like? How does a verbal insult damage us, particularly when we are children?

3. What is the place of forgiveness in reconciliation? Read Matthew 18:15–35. Is there help here for the whole process of dealing with conflict in a congregation and the importance of forgiveness?

4. Does dividing this passage (Matthew 5:21–26) into "Traditional Righteousness," "The Vicious Cycle," and "The Transforming Initiative" help you better understand this first discipleship commandment to

---

8. Kreider, *Patient Ferment*, 216–17, 219, 234–35. Reconciliation before the Eucharist and worship in the early church also involved the kiss of peace.

reconcile? Think of other creative, transforming initiatives that can help your relationships this coming week.

Prayer Thought

Loving God, my anger gets in the way. My impatience is a problem. I often see things only from my point of view and my own self-interests. Give me the grace to see things from the point of view of my partner in conflict. Above all, help me see things in your loving, just, and forgiving ways. Amen.

8

Discipleship Commandment 2: Deal with Lust!

Traditional Righteousness	The Vicious Cycle	Transforming Initiative
Matthew 5:27— "You have heard that it was said, 'You shall not commit adultery.'"	[28] But I say to you that everyone who looks at a woman with lust has already committed adultery with her in his heart.	[29] If your right eye causes you to sin, tear it out and throw it away; it is better for you to lose one of your members than for your whole body to be thrown into hell. [30] And if your right hand causes you to sin, cut it off and throw it away; it is better for you to lose one of your members than for your whole body to go into hell.

Sexual desire is a wonderful, lovely gift from God. Misdirected or misused, however, it can become a betrayal of our partner. "You shall not commit adultery" is one of the Ten Commandments.[1] What is Jesus teaching here?

Jesus has in mind actually two of the Ten Commandments:

    No. 7   You shall not commit adultery.
    No. 10   You shall not covet your neighbor's . . . wife.[2]

---

1. Exodus 20:14 and Deuteronomy 5:18.
2. Exodus 19:14, 17; Deuteronomy 5:18, 21.

Part Two | Sermon on the Mount

Jesus is thus repeating the message of the Ten Commandments:

> No. 7   Don't do it!
> No. 10 Don't think about doing it!

Do not covet someone else sexually. All sins arise from the sin of covetousness, including the seeking of power over another.[3] Jesus' teachings here about unfaithful lust (sexual desire) are strong. His vivid language gets our attention. Tear out your eye means do not look! Cutting off your hand means do not touch!

We don't understand it literally that we should cut off our right hand, or tear out our eye, or anything else ... but what about the lustful thought? What about books, magazines, TV programs, films, or videos that promote sexual desire? Should they be cut out?

Note that Jesus is not teaching against the sexual attraction between two who have covenanted together before God to live faithfully for life. That joy is intended and planned by God. Our sexuality is a God-given gift. Such sexual love, with friendship and faithfulness to each other, creates a strong marriage. Tender intimacy truly is lovemaking, love-creating. In the Gospel of Mark, Jesus quotes the first chapter of Genesis in the creation of Adam and Eve:

> But from the beginning of creation, "God made them male and female ... For this reason a man shall leave his father and mother and be joined to his wife, and the two shall become one flesh." So they are no longer two, but one flesh. Therefore, what God has joined together, let no one separate.[4]

Jesus thus celebrates and prizes human sexuality, and speaks of its beauty and purity, intended from the beginning of creation. Today not all Christians have the same opinion about homosexual relationships, but the principle of fidelity and purity can apply here as well.

What though of adultery? While Jesus is clear about the importance of faithfulness, it is also important to remember the story of Jesus' encounter with the woman caught in adultery in John 8.[5] Important background to this story is that according to Leviticus 20:10 adultery was to be punished by the death penalty: both the man and the woman were to be put to death. In the story in the Gospel of John, the crowd brought the woman to Jesus

---

3. Ellul, *If You Are the Son of God*, 10–12.
4. Mark 10:6–9.
5. John 8:2–11.

for a verdict; the woman was "caught in the very act of adultery." Jesus' response is simply to write in the sand. This gave time for emotions to cool, for the thinking part of the brain to start functioning. Then Jesus eventually asked for anyone without sin to throw the first stone. The people in the crowd went away one by one, the oldest first, until only the woman was left. It is important to note that the adulterous man was not brought before Jesus for judgement. But Jesus does not ask for him either. Jesus simply said to the woman that he did not condemn her, and that she should not sin again. Here justice and mercy meet. Jesus' judgement is a saving judgement, not one of condemnation or death by stoning. Jesus grants a fresh, new beginning, with a loving invitation to not sin again.

Evolutionarily, we are simply wired for sex. Those that copulate pass on their genes. But in human communities our sexual instincts are better channeled in constructive ways. Wise behavior reduces conflict, jealousy, and builds trust in community. So, noticing our lust, taking practical steps to deal with it, and making wiser choices prevents problems like family breakdown and crimes of passion.[6]

REFLECTIONS

1. French Christian and intellectual Jacques Ellul wrote, "Covetousness is the source of all sins." He also states that it is also the root of seeking to possess and have power over another. How are we to deal with sexual covetousness?[7] What practical things can we do to safeguard our own integrity and that of others? Why is it so difficult?
2. What is a healthy theology of sex for Christians?
3. What boundaries can we put in place to keep us safer from the sin of sexual covetousness?

Prayer Thought

Help me, loving God, to strategically tackle the roots of sexual temptation before they lead me and others into great danger. Amen.

---

6. Author conversation with James Rathbone. James also commented that there are further nuances to perhaps be explored here.

7. Ellul, *If You Are the Son of God*, 10–12.

9

Discipleship Commandment 3: Honor Marriage!

Traditional Righteousness	The Vicious Cycle	Transforming Initiative
Matthew 5:31—"It was also said, 'Whoever divorces his wife, let him give her a certificate of divorce.'"	³² But I say to you that anyone who divorces his wife, except on the ground of unchastity, causes her to commit adultery; and whoever marries a divorced woman commits adultery.	[Not in the passage. Helped by 1 Corinthians 7:10–11. Perhaps the missing text could read: Go, first be reconciled to your spouse.]

WHAT MIGHT JESUS BE SAYING ABOUT DIVORCE?

The first thing to say is that Jesus challenges patriarchal norms. Here he is telling men to treat their wives justly. I once did a study of stories of Jesus interacting with women in the Gospels. I learned that women always had a voice and sometimes Jesus even provoked them to speak what they were really thinking. In all these encounters with Jesus I found women walked away with new dignity.

Domestic violence is an issue. Jewell, my spouse, at one time worked in a women's refuge. She learned that it took an abused woman up to thirty-five attempts before she finally left an abusive partner for safety. A theologian friend, speaking out of her personal experience, thought verbal abuse and violence was a form of unchastity, an awful breaking of covenant. Thus, I personally believe a woman should get out of an abusive relationship without guilt.

Now, let us first look at the Torah background to this discipleship commandment. Divorce was permitted among the Israelites, but only for men, according to Deuteronomy 24:1–2.[1] Malachi, in the last book of the Old Testament, argues thus for the rights of women: "So look to yourselves, and do not let anyone be faithless to the wife of his youth. For I hate divorce, says the Lord, the God of Israel . . ."[2] When Jesus is asked later in Matthew why Moses permitted divorce, his reply echoes the prophet Malachi and the story of Adam and Eve: "It was because you were so hard-hearted that Moses allowed you to divorce your wives, but from the beginning it was not so."[3]

The point being made by Malachi is that it was wrong for a middle-aged man to dump the wife of his youth, and then marry a younger woman, particularly when it was only the man who could seek divorce. A woman at this time had no right in Jewish law to seek divorce. To divorce a wife, then, would also mean economic hardship, poverty, and destitution for her, as it does for many women today. Jesus is clearly against this injustice. This concern about divorce is continued in the early church in Paul's Letter to the Corinthians.[4] Jesus also adds that in the beginning, marriage was meant to be an enduring, equal, loving, and faithful relationship. However, he does allow divorce on the grounds of unchastity in this Sermon on the Mount passage.

In Matthew 19, on the blessing of children, Jesus' actual blessing of the children[5] comes immediately after he speaks about divorce.[6] It is not an accident of positioning these two passages together, given Jesus' high regard for children. The implication of this passage from Matthew, and identical passages in Luke and Mark, is that marriages should bless the children. The

---

1. For an alternative view see David Instone-Brewer, *Divorce and Remarriage in the Bible*. He argues that women sometimes did divorce their husbands for neglect, based on rabbinic understanding of Exodus 21:10–11. The rabbinic argument was that if this applied to a slave, then even more so it applied to a wife who was not a slave.
2. Malachi 2:15–16.
3. Matthew 19:8.
4. Corinthians 7:10–11.
5. Matthew 19:13–15.
6. Matthew 19:2–12.

needs of children should challenge the selfishness of the marriage partners. Again, a little child shall lead us, as seen in the passage of Isaiah 11:6.

Given Jesus' high standards regarding marriage, what might Jesus say to a divorced person today? There is an important story of Jesus encountering a Samaritan woman at the well in John 4:1–42. First of all, note that the Samaritan woman was alone at the well and getting her water at noon. Normally the women of the village would meet at the well early in the morning before it was too hot. It was a communal event, with women meeting and chatting together. This Samaritan woman seems to have been excluded from such village fellowship.

Second, remember the social hierarchy of the day. Many Jews saw themselves as superior to Samaritans, and men often saw themselves above women. Jesus, however, in asking for a drink of water, puts himself below this Samaritan woman. In the ensuing conversation, the surprised Samaritan woman is also promised living water that Jesus can gift her with. The woman banters back. Jesus asks her to bring her husband, and she says she has no husband. Then comes the loving confrontation from Jesus, who tells her she has had five husbands, and the man she is currently living with is not her husband. It is no wonder that this woman, a possible five-time divorcée and currently living unmarried with yet another man, was excluded for this reason by the other women of the village.

For her part, the Samaritan woman has been involuntarily divorced by five men. Imagine her tears, her heartbreak, and now her loneliness as she is rejected also by the women of her village. However, Jesus does not condemn her, but promises her living water so she will not thirst again. The loving Spirit of God will satisfy her spiritual hunger, the hole in her soul. She comes to understand that Jesus is the Messiah, and she goes to all the villagers to tell of her experience. Others believe. Jesus stays for two more days. The woman is restored to the fellowship of the village. Her story is still told.

This story suggests that in Christ, the divorced person can find healing for his or her soul, the empty places can be filled by God's loving Spirit, and he or she can find a place again among God's people.

WHAT MAKES FOR A SUCCESSFUL MARRIAGE?

This is an important question. Prevention of the breakdown of marriage is better than trying to get over divorce. I share from my own pastoral

Discipleship Commandment 3: Honor Marriage!

experience in Britain, the USA, and Asia. You will have important insights too from your own experience and reflections. My thoughts are thus exploratory, and not the last word.

First step. Choose a partner carefully! Do not be hasty! Have common goals. Both partners being disciples of Jesus and committed to Christ's mission is really helpful. Serving the purposes of God's kingdom takes us out of ourselves; there is no greater goal in life than for two people to pray and work together for the kingdom of heaven on earth.

Then prepare for marriage thoroughly. Start talking early about things that matter to each other. It is really important to talk and plan about finances, because this can be a big stressor in a marriage. Do you both want children? Conversations about intimacy are an important part of good communication. Premarital counseling helps these and other important conversations to happen. Violence, or the threat of violence, is a big red warning light in courtship.

Start premarital counseling at least six months before the wedding so you have time to change your mind. Marriage preparations can acquire a speed that is difficult to slow or stop. Taking more time can prevent an unwise marriage.

Marriage involves expressions of commitment. It is a meaningful and foundational step for two people to share personally, with each other, that they love one another. It is a further significant step to make lifetime promises to each other publicly before family and friends, in a legal ceremony of marriage. To do this means you are really serious! Finally, to also make such promises before God, inviting God's Spirit to be a partner in the marriage, is to make marriage a sacrament, a covenant. Marriage is then a three-stranded commitment: personal, legal, and sacramental. All three dimensions are important.

We have been talking about marriage. However, some feel the calling to singleness. We should remember that both Jesus and Paul, and many others since, have lived full and meaningful lives of joyful service in this way.

Jesus' teaching on marriage and divorce could be summarized as follows: Jesus' followers should have a new heart that calls both partners to live out a new kind of relationship, an equal and mutual partnership, the kind that was intended in the beginning of creation. Marriage is an expression of discipleship in Christian community together; it is to be a mini-communal expression of the kingdom of God. A marriage is to be a team for Jesus, and for the mission of Jesus. By grace, this is possible for all humans, whether heterosexual or homosexual. By such a marriage children and many others will be blessed.

In the Sermon on the Mount, there is no transforming initiative described. Stassen was helped by Paul to suggest that the missing transforming initiative could read: "Go, first be reconciled to your spouse."[7]

Go, first be reconciled to your spouse! Every marriage has problems. Address them. Work them out, if at all possible, remembering that abuse and unfaithfulness are possible grounds for divorce. Get skilled help. Reconcile and forgive. Forgiveness is an essential part of marriage. I am so grateful for my wife, Jewell's, regular loving confrontation, for I am often wrong. It is her unstinting and rapid forgiveness that helps restore our relationship.

REFLECTIONS

1. What do you think makes for a loving and mutual marriage? Is there a tension between your ideas and this passage in Matthew 5:31–32?
2. What does it mean to bring a marriage under the blessing and guidance of the Spirit of Jesus? How might this bless the marriage partners, any children, and others?
3. Is verbal and physical abuse in a marriage a form of unfaithfulness, and just as serious as adultery? What do you think?
4. How can a Christian community support faithful, mutual marriage? How can a congregation help a struggling marriage find reconciliation and renewal?

Prayer Thought

Loving God, help us choose wisely, if called to marriage. Help us honor our own marriages, forgiving and reconciling with each other justly and fairly. Bless those who choose singleness, and help me respect and support the relationships of others. Grant us grace, reconciliation, and wisdom. Amen.

---

7. 1 Corinthians 7:10–11. Stassen, "Fourteen Triads," 277. Stassen suggested "wife" originally. I have substituted "spouse."

10

Discipleship Commandment 4: Tell the Truth!

Traditional Righteousness	The Vicious Cycle	Transforming Initiative
Matthew 5:33— "Again, you have heard that it was said to those of ancient times, 'You shall not swear falsely, but carry out the vows you have made to the Lord.'"	[34] But I say to you, Do not swear at all, either by heaven, for it is the throne of God, [35] or by the earth, for it is his footstool, or by Jerusalem, for it is the city of the great King. [36] And do not swear by your head, for you cannot make one hair white or black.	[37] Let your word be "Yes, Yes" or "No, No"; anything more than this comes from the evil one.

> Above all, my beloved, do not swear, either by heaven or by earth or by any other oath, but let your "Yes" be yes and your "No" be no, so that you may not fall under condemnation.
> (James 5:12)

Let your yes be yes and your no be no! This is the message of the Sermon on the Mount and the Letter of James above. Disciples are to tell the truth all the time. They then do not need to swear an oath to say they are telling the truth in one instance. This discredits what they say the rest of the time. Disciples are to be consistently honest in their speech. This creates trust, and trust makes for authentic community and peace. Truth-telling is a transforming initiative, whereas untruthfulness creates a vicious cycle. Again, truthfulness builds healthy community.

Behind this teaching of Jesus are two of the Ten Commandments: "You shall not make wrongful use of the name of the LORD your God"[1] and "You shall not bear false witness against your neighbor."[2] In addition, truth-telling is commanded in a passage in Leviticus that includes non-retaliation and love of enemies.[3]

To tell the truth about others is also a legal requirement. For instance, slander, defamation, and libel can be confronted in court action, and perjury can carry a prison sentence.

Disciples of Jesus are to avoid all forms of lying. But what about gossip, stereotyping, jokes about other ethnic groups, and prejudice? These are also forms of bearing false witness, of being untruthful. The sin here is that it dehumanizes others, permits mistreatment, and even incites and justifies killing. The Holocaust in World War II was the culmination of centuries of false witness by Christians against Jews. The fruit of false witness can be terror.

Fake news stories lie about current events. Fake news can discredit sound medical practices like vaccinations, so parents are scared to inoculate their children, thus creating, for example, a measles epidemic. Fake news can be an accusation made by a politician to discredit truthful and responsible media reporting that may be rightly critical of a politician. Fake news may be untruthful statements by populist politicians about an ethnic minority. This can increase hate crimes by the majority against a vulnerable minority, perhaps Muslims, or Jews, or immigrants, or black people. Untruthfulness or fake news can lead to division and violence.

Conspiracy theories about politics, minority groups like Jews or Muslims, or scientifically tested health measures like vaccines and fluoridation of water can also be forms of lying and propaganda that can kill people. This kind of conspiracy theory (that cannot be, or has not been tested, and that is based on dubious science or historical research) is better called "conspiracy fictions."[4]

It is said that truth is the first casualty in war. Censorship and government propaganda can distort the news so that the whole population of a

---

1. Exodus 20:7; Deuteronomy 5:11.
2. Exodus 20:16; Deuteronomy 5:20.
3. Leviticus 19:12–18.
4. Monbiot, "World According to Jason," 35.

Discipleship Commandment 4: Tell the Truth!

nation is lied to. Only after the war, through the efforts of academic historians, may the truth of what really happened come out. War was declared against Iraq in 2003 on the pretext the nation had weapons of mass destruction. No such weapons were ever found, but it is responsibly reported by the Iraq Body Count Project that a total of 300,000 people have died since the 2003 invasion, two-thirds of whom were civilians.[5] And this is probably an underestimate.[6]

There is also fake history. Patriotic history is often dishonest history, excusing ourselves, demonizing the other, and this can lead to genocide. To be a disciple of Jesus is to also be committed to be honest in the writing, reading, and interpreting of history.

Discernment, listening to the Holy Spirit in our decision-making processes, has to also check the reliability of fact claims. If our decision-making process includes misleading information, then our conclusions will be in error. Truthfulness matters!

The seventh article of the 1527 Anabaptist Schleitheim Confession forbids oath-making on the grounds that Jesus forbade it. It follows the sixth article against the sword.[7] The Schleitheim Confession is recognized as a foundational document by Mennonites, Hutterites, and other Anabaptists.

George Fox and other early Quakers refused to swear on the Bible in court. The Bible itself prohibits swearing in this Sermon on the Mount passage. Early Quakers also refused to make oaths of loyalty to the ruler, be it Oliver Cromwell or Charles II, and were often sent to prison for refusing. They simply affirmed that they were telling the truth. Consistent truth-telling is a continuing part of Quaker commitment to nonviolence today.

Scholars consider this tradition of truth telling to be very early in the Christian tradition.[8] Robert Guelich succinctly puts the reason for its importance as follows: "The prohibition of oaths and the demand that simply one's word stand for itself is nothing less than to demand a relationship between individuals characterized by total honesty."[9]

---

5. Iraq Body Count.
6. See "Costs of War Project" at the Brown University in Rhode Island for an update.
7. "Schleitheim Confession."
8. See for instance in Kreider, *Patient Ferment*, Origen teaching catechumens against oath making, 174; martyr Phileas refusing to swear, 250. Although eventually a Christian, the Emperor Constantine, through an edict in 334, legislated oath-taking despite the strong Christian tradition going back to Jesus against this practice. Later, Augustine argued for "'just oaths', compromising the church further," 271–72.
9. Guelich, *Sermon on the Mount*, 250.

Truth without love cuts; love without truth betrays. In our personal interactions, truth and untruth can be weapons to injure one another. The following verse from Ephesians is good counsel: "But speaking the truth in love, we must grow up in every way into him who is the head, into Christ."[10]

Mahatma Gandhi pioneered "truth force" (*satyagraha*) in his nonviolent resistance of British racism and colonial rule in South Africa and India. Truth for Gandhi was rooted in love, but he was insistent that the truthful reality of oppression and injustice should be faced and civilly resisted in nonviolent ways.

But what if telling the truth threatens an innocent person? Suppose you were hiding a Jew when the Nazis came knocking on your door? Is protecting life more important than being truthful? Is silence an option?

Finally, Jesus also said "When the Spirit of truth comes, he will guide you into all the truth . . ." (John 16:13). Likewise, untruthfulness is demonic and murderous (John 8:44). To be truthful is our response to the truthfulness of God's loving Spirit. Then we participate in the life of God, the honest, authentic kingdom life.

Let our yes be yes, and our no be no!

REFLECTIONS

1. We are often tempted to tell small white lies to ease our social relationships. Do white lies still betray both the command of Jesus to be truthful, and in the long run compromise our relationships with others? When caught in a white lie, is not trust broken? If trust is broken, is it difficult to repair? What is your experience?

2. Is a way forward sometimes to say, "I cannot answer that question fully at this time, so I am not going to say anything because I do not want to lie to you"?

3. Does Jesus use silence? Is silence within the spirit of Jesus' teachings, or is it also a compromise?

4. To what extent is lying evading responsibility and accountability?

5. How does being truthful help create both justice and peace? If governments lie to their citizens, how is the kingdom of God to be different?

---

10. Ephesians 4:15.

Discipleship Commandment 4: Tell the Truth!

Prayer Thought

Loving, truthful God, give me courage to always tell the truth, and love and wisdom to tell it rightly. Amen.

11

Discipleship Commandment 5: No Retaliation!

Traditional Righteousness	The Vicious Cycle	Transforming Initiative
Matthew 5:38—"You have heard that it was said, 'An eye for an eye and a tooth for a tooth.'"	[39] But I say to you, Do not resist an evildoer.	But if anyone strikes you on the right cheek, turn the other also; [40] and if anyone wants to sue you and take your coat, give your cloak as well; [41] and if anyone forces you to go one mile, go also the second mile. [42] Give to everyone who begs from you, and do not refuse anyone who wants to borrow from you.

When you are hurt by someone, is your first instinct to retaliate? When you are hurt by someone, do you get mad, get even, or get ahead? Is Jesus saying here that you should let others walk all over you? Let us look more closely.

"You have heard that it was said, 'An eye for an eye and a tooth for a tooth.'" Jesus is referring to the law of retaliation that is described three times in the Old Testament.[1] Actually, the law of retaliation was intended to

---

1. Exodus 21:23–25, Leviticus 24:17–21, and Deuteronomy 19:21.

Discipleship Commandment 5: No Retaliation!

limit revenge, and this was progress. But Jesus took it further by ruling out retaliation altogether when he said do not resist an evildoer.

What does it mean, "Do not resist an evildoer"? First of all, these words are a shock to our imagination. I am helped by Dorothy Jean Weaver to dig deeper by reading her book *The Irony of Power,* and incorporate some of her ideas in the following, in addition to those of Walter Wink and others.

It is helpful to look at Deuteronomy 19:19–21 that Jesus is actually quoting. Verse 19 ends "And you shall remove the evil one from your midst." This is actually to be done by capital punishment, "life for life . . ." (verse 21). Jesus instead has a different and creative strategy.

First of all, it is important to remember that Jesus resisted evil in numerous stories in the four Gospels. Later in Matthew he talks about the importance of not neglecting "the weightier matters of the law: justice and mercy and faith."[2] So Jesus is not giving up on justice. The disciples of Jesus are to also resist evil/injustice, but also to remember justice with mercy and faith. We are to resist evil, but at the same time love the evildoer. For example, by turning the other cheek, surrendering our cloak as well as our shirt in court, walking the second mile with a Roman soldier, and lending to whoever asks for help. The evil one is not to be executed, or assassinated, but challenged creatively by a gracious, unexpected, and surprising response.[3]

Retaliation can lead to a vicious cycle that dramatically escalates a conflict by increasing fear, anger, and fight or flight. This is true in a marriage or in war. At this time of writing, the Russia/Ukraine war is raging, and many are fearful that it could escalate to an utterly terrifying nuclear war through retaliation.

Jesus has thus ruled out retaliation. Jesus instead is outlining a redemptive option, a strategy that softens and then wins the heart of the evil one. Let us look at Jesus' transforming initiatives further, and see how they contrast and replace the retaliation option. In the following I am helped by Walter Wink's work.[4]

If someone strikes you on your right cheek, it means they are hitting you with the back of their right hand. This was a blow by a right-handed person, who is a "superior," to put you, an "inferior," in your place. It is an insult intended to demean you. If you turn your head, to present your

---

2. Matthew 23:23.
3. See Weaver, *Irony of Power*, 137–74.
4. Wink, *Engaging the Powers*, 175–84.

Part Two | Sermon on the Mount

left cheek as Jesus says, the "superior" person can no longer hit you with the back of their right hand without hitting your teeth and thereby injuring their own hand. You confuse the "superior" person. He wonders, what should he do now? So you are creatively resisting, but without retaliation.

A Roman soldier could command a Jewish peasant to carry his pack for one mile, but not two. Roman army regulations, like army regulations today, were strict. There were clear mile markers on Roman roads in their occupied countries. By carrying the soldier's pack a second mile, the disciple is confusing the soldier. The soldier might be glad that you, a stupid Jewish peasant, are still carrying his pack. But he might also be worried that he could get in trouble for breaking strict army regulations. The disciple is asserting that he has a choice, he is choosing to be gracious, hospitable, and kind, but he is also creatively resisting the Roman occupation, using relational power. The conversation is now different over the second mile, and the status of peasant is also different.

Psychologically, when Jesus rules out retaliation, this reduces fear and de-escalates a conflict. In suggesting creative, assertive, intelligent responses, we move from animal anger to human creative thinking. Assertive behavior is neither servile nor domineering, and has the best chance of getting a positive response from the other person, but it of course does not guarantee this. Nevertheless, Gandhi and Martin Luther King Jr., who both took the discipline of the Sermon on the Mount seriously, were effective in their assertive, nonviolent resistance to oppression. Game theory based on the prisoner's dilemma is also interesting to explore. Strategies that forgive, challenge when cheated, and that are nice, clear, and easy to trust, come out top. Nasty, selfish strategies do not work well. Cooperation pays.[5]

Debt was a big problem for the poor in Jesus' day, and a creditor could take a poor person to court to get even the debtor's shirt as part payment of the loan. Jesus is saying in this situation give your "coat" as well.[6] This actually meant you were now naked in court. In Jewish culture, shame belongs to the one who sees someone naked, not the person who is naked. So, by giving your coat, you expose the injustice of the court system that has so meanly already taken your shirt. You have resisted, protested creatively, but again without retaliation.

---

5. Author conversation with James Rathbone. Also see "What Game Theory Reveals About Life, The Universe, and Everything."

6. Matthew 5:40. The New Internationalist Version uses "shirt" and "coat," making it clear that it is the inner and outer clothing that is being surrendered. The King James and the New Revised Standard Version uses "coat" and "cloak," which is a little confusing.

Discipleship Commandment 5: No Retaliation!

Jesus is really saying we should resist creatively, nonviolently, without retaliation, without killing or injuring the evildoer as mandated in Deuteronomy 19:19–21. Wink says, "Do not resist an evildoer" (verse 39a) really means "Do not repay evil for evil."[7] Adin Ballou, a nineteenth-century American, compiled a "Catechism of Non-Resistance" that contains a remarkably clear interpretation of the meaning of this passage:

> Question: Ought the word "non-resistance" to be taken in its widest sense—that is to say, as intending that we should not offer any resistance of any kind to evil?
> Answer: No; it ought to be taken in the exact sense of our Saviour's teaching—that is, not repaying evil for evil. We ought to oppose evil by every righteous means in our power, but not by evil.[8]

Thus, to work against injustice by nonviolent means is right, indeed a responsibility of a disciple. The active, nonviolent resistance of Gandhi and Martin Luther King Jr. is much closer to the meaning of this passage than do-nothing pacifism. And as King said, "The old law of an eye for an eye leaves everybody blind!"[9] Jesus is giving disciples of the kingdom a different, creative, nonviolent way to redemptively resist oppressive social structures and empire.

Jews exercised two strategies in response to Roman colonization. One was collaboration with the Romans. Collaborators, who profited from the Roman occupation, were of course hated as traitors. The other strategy was violent revolt against the Romans—freedom fighters. Jesus decisively rejected both. Collaboration with evil was not the kingdom way. Matthew's gospel was written after the failure of the recent Jewish revolt of 66–70 CE and the destruction of the temple and Jerusalem. This was a stark warning about the danger and ineffectiveness of violent revolution to the author of Matthew and his audience.

Is this teaching on non-retaliation only found here in the Sermon on the Mount? Actually, no. Gordon Zerbe, a Canadian New Testament scholar, has found over thirty New Testament passages that witness to some form of non-retaliation, including not cursing, not going to court, forbearing, enduring, and being at peace.[10] Willard Swartley sums up this argument as follows:

---

7. Wink, *Engaging the Powers*, 184–86.
8. Ballou, cited in Tolstoy, *Kingdom of God*, 11.
9. King, *Words of Martin Luther King*, 59.
10. Cited in Swartley, *Covenant of Peace*, 409.

> The consistency of the New Testament's ethical stance of non-retaliation to evil is striking, for it presents the gospel's solution to the [dominance] of . . . violence in human culture. Nowhere does the New Testament condone the use of violence by Christ's followers, even as a means to defeat evil.[11]

Around 3,000 people died in the 9/11 tragedy. The American-led coalition of revenge inflicted a far greater human cost. According to the Costs of War Project at Brown University, the wider USA-led war on terror, twenty years after 9/11, has cost $8 trillion, over 940,000 deaths due to direct war violence, plus an estimated 3.6–3.8 million indirectly, with 432,000 civilians killed. The number of war refugees and displaced persons totals 38 million. At least four times the number of US soldiers killed in combat have sadly died from suicide,[12] with great emotional cost to their families.

As my mum taught my brothers and me, "Two wrongs do not make a right!"

REFLECTIONS

1. Have I suffered from retaliation? Have I retaliated? In each case what happened? Was it a solution to the initial wrong?

2. Hitting back is strongly ingrained in us. Parents sometimes encourage their children to do this at school. What about novels and films? How does popular culture perhaps encourage retaliation?

3. How have you seen creative resistance/non-retaliation work? What happened?

4. The Austro-Hungarian Empire launched an attack on Serbia in retaliation for the assassination of Archduke Ferdinand in 1914. Thus began the disastrous World War I, which has been called the founding catastrophe of the twentieth century. Can you think of any other examples of disastrous retaliations in history, or in your life, that spiraled out of control?

---

11. Swartley, *Covenant of Peace*, 428.
12. "Costs of War Project."

Discipleship Commandment 5: No Retaliation!

Prayer Thought

Crucified Jesus, help me not retaliate. Help me to assert my dignity and the dignity of the other person by addressing the wrong creatively. Help me find ways to end and heal injustice nonviolently. Amen.

12

Discipleship Commandment 6: Love Your Enemies!

Traditional Righteousness	The Vicious Cycle	Transforming Initiative
Matthew 5:43— "You have heard that it was said, 'You shall love your neighbour and hate your enemy.'"		[44] But I say to you, Love your enemies and pray for those who persecute you, [45] so that you may be children of your Father in heaven; for he makes his sun rise on the evil and on the good, and sends rain on the righteous and on the unrighteous.
	[46] For if you love those who love you, what reward do you have? Do not even the tax-collectors do the same? [47] And if you greet only your brothers and sisters, what more are you doing than others? Do not even the Gentiles do the same?	[48] Be perfect, therefore, as your heavenly Father is perfect.

Discipleship Commandment 6: Love Your Enemies!

Jesus' teaching sounds like good news for enemies! Is it also good news for disciples? While love may not always transform an enemy into a friend, does hate always corrupt the hater? Can one be a disciple of Jesus and hate?

"Love your neighbor as yourself" is found in Leviticus 19:18. "Hate your enemy" is not actually a biblical quote. It was more a common folk saying in the time of Jesus. There are examples in the Hebrew Scriptures of loving your enemy, and Dale Allison points out two examples.[1] One is David not killing Saul, even when Saul is seeking to kill him.[2] A further example are these commands:

> When you come upon your enemy's ox or donkey going astray, you shall bring it back. When you see the donkey of one who hates you lying under its burden and you would hold back from setting it free, you must help to set it free.[3]

When Jesus is teaching "Love your enemies," he is strengthening an existing Jewish tradition.

An inspiring French friend, Jean Bouissou, tells this story:

> A few years ago, I had an enriching experience in Paris. After a course in human relations which finished around 11:00 p.m., I was hungry because I had not had my evening meal. I drove to the only restaurant open all night, next to the Arch of Triumph. The only dish they were serving at this late hour was a shrimp salad. As I was about to eat, sitting alone in the large room, two young men stormed into the restaurant. They had long hair and unorthodox clothes. They looked aggressive. They came and sat across the table from me. While they stared at me, one of them took a fork and helped himself to shrimp from my dish. I remained silent and just smiled. Then we had this conversation:
>
> "Aren't you angry at us eating your shrimp?"
>
> "Not really, you are about the age of my own sons and you remind me of them."
>
> "Why don't you yell at us? Why don't you call the attendant or the police?"
>
> "If my sons were acting as you are, I would like the people they disturb to show a little patience and understanding. After all, I don't know what kind of misdeeds my boys do when they go out by themselves at night!"

---

1. Allison Jr., *Sermon on the Mount*, 100.
2. 1 Samuel 24:1–18.
3. Exodus 23:4–5.

They stopped eating and excused themselves.

"Sir, we are really sorry for the inconvenience. If we were rude, it is because we have been refused entrance in several restaurants earlier this evening."

"Why?"

"Our dress and hairstyle are not generally accepted in this area. We arrived by train from the country this afternoon. It is our first evening in Paris."

"So you must be both hungry and angry?"

"Yes. In fact we decided that this would be the last restaurant that would refuse us. We were ready to break jaws and furniture had we been asked to leave."

"What are you guys doing in Paris?"

"We had an argument with our father at the farm. He is a dictator. He feels we should work for him without much pay. We came to Paris to find work and be more independent."

"I wish you good success, boys!"

"Sir, if our father had been like you, we would never have left the farm."

I ordered another dish, and we talked further before parting as good friends.[4]

Martin Luther King Jr. said this:

> The nonviolent approach does not immediately change the heart of the oppressor. It first does something to the hearts and souls of those committed to it. It gives them new self-respect; it calls up resources of strength and courage that they did not know they had. Finally, it reaches the opponent and so stirs [their] conscience that reconciliation becomes a reality.[5]

Jean Bouissou's marvelous story illustrates the truth of King's words, written in the middle of the hatred and violence of vicious white racists/segregationists during the US civil rights movement (1954–1968).

There is another reason we should love our enemies. There is good and evil in all of us. To love our enemies is also to cry for mercy for ourselves. Praying for my enemies is the first step in softening my heart. It is our loving actions that soften the hearts of our enemies. Why, according to Jesus, should we love our enemies?

---

4. Bouissou, *Christ and Community*, 110–12.
5. King, *Words of Martin Luther King*, 65–66.

Discipleship Commandment 6: Love Your Enemies!

"So that you may be children of your Father in heaven; for he makes his sun rise on the evil and on the good, and sends rain on the righteous and on the unrighteous."[6]

Sunshine and rain enable crops to grow. God, out of love, wants all to be fed, whether good or bad. God is a God of grace for all.

This passage ends with Jesus concluding, "Be perfect, therefore, as your heavenly Father is perfect."[7] In the parallel verse in the Sermon on the Plain in Luke's Gospel it reads, "Be merciful, just as your Father is merciful."[8] We are to be perfect in mercy to our enemies. God's perfect mercy is revealed in the crucifixion as Jesus cries out a prayer, "Father, forgive them; for they do not know what they are doing."[9]

"Father" is used for God four times in Mark, twenty-nine times in Luke, and an astonishing forty-two times in Matthew.[10] It is actually used seventeen times in Matthew's Sermon on the Mount, nearly half the occurrences—in just three chapters out of the twenty-eight chapters in Matthew. "Father," of course, is patriarchal language, but what is the character of the "Father" in the Sermon on the Mount? *Our Father in heaven* is first of all a nurturing, loving parent of all—"he makes his sun rise on the evil and on the good, and sends rain on the righteous and on the unrighteous."[11] Our Father is perfect in mercy. And if we are commanded to love our enemies, then we do so because God first loves God's enemies.

At Jesus' birth, he is named Emmanuel, "God is with us."[12] Jesus shows us what God is like, the Son reveals the Father's character—healer, blesser of children, advocate for the poor and vulnerable, the crucified God. In the Lord's Prayer, whatever our ethnicity, gender, sexual orientation, or age, we join together and say "*Our* Father . . ." "Father" is relational language, the language of loving intimacy and closeness in Matthew. As already mentioned, Father is patriarchal language, but in Matthew's Gospel it has a deeply subversive content. The Father in heaven is not like a boss-husband, or a dictator-dad. Nor is Father in heaven like Herod the Great, Herod the

---

6. Matthew 5:45.
7. Matthew 5:48.
8. Luke 6:38.
9. Luke 23:34.
10. Bredin, *Jesus, Revolutionary of the Poor*, 24n26. Bredin says Father is used times and also three times. Checking elsewhere, it seems to be four times.
11. Matthew 5:45.
12. Matthew 1:23.

Tetrarch, Pilate, or Caesar; and the upside-down kingdom of heaven is not at all like the Roman Empire. Yang summarizes this point well: "In Matthew, then, the Father in heaven has a political connotation. Against the emperor's image of an oppressive and exploitative father, Matthew paints an image of God as the true father, who loves and protects his children with grace."[13]

"Love your enemies" is the hardest commandment of Jesus, but it is his most important one. As a soldier is trained to be violent, so we have to be trained to practice enemy love. Our instincts are not to love our enemies, the animal part of our brain is wired for fear of danger and fight or flight. For the lunch counter sit-ins in the American civil rights movement, James Lawson insisted on rigorous nonviolent training of participants to cope with the abuse the protestors received, so their witness was not compromised by outbursts of retaliation.[14]

Jesus models love of enemies from the cross, with the words, "Father forgive them for they know not what they do."[15] This takes us to the heart of the good news of God's grace for all. No matter what we have done, God forgives us and grants us an ever fresh and new beginning. We are called to do the same for others.

REFLECTIONS

1. Who are your enemies? Why and how is it difficult to love them?

2. Are we enemies of God? How does God treat God's enemies, according to this passage? How then are we to treat our enemies?

3. How does Jesus demonstrate God's love of enemies in the Gospel stories?

4. The early Christians had a consistent life ethic—no abortion, infanticide, or child exposure. Early Christians were against gladiatorial games, against the death penalty, and if in the army could not kill. Should the church today have a consistent life ethic also? Is abortion a particularly difficult question?

13. Yang, "Sermon on the Mount/Plain," 848.

14. Chávez-Nava and Codilla, "60 Years Ago Today." Author conversation with James Rathbone.

15. Luke 23:34.

Discipleship Commandment 6: Love Your Enemies!

5. Is standing up to our enemies in pursuit of justice, like Gandhi and Martin Luther King Jr. did, a form of loving our enemies? How?
6. How does forgiveness play a role in loving our enemies?
7. In World Wars I and II in Europe, Catholics shot Catholics and Protestants bayonetted Protestants. As we move to post-Christendom times, what should churches be saying about Christians serving in the armed forces of their country?

Prayer Thought

Write down your current enemies. Begin now to pray for them and continue to do so, adding any new names to your list.

13

Six Discipleship Commandments: Some Conclusions

Peacemaking "Jesus-style" is comprehensive, holistic. Disciples of Jesus are to learn how to make peace with one another in the fellowship of the church. They deal with anger and do not use the courts. Disciples keep the peace of marriage—a communal expression of the kingdom of God. They deal with lust and other temptations of selfish injustice against a partner to keep marriage faithful, loving, and true. Disciples are honest; they tell the truth. Their consistency in truth-telling builds trust with others. Disciples do not retaliate in situations of oppression and injustice, but resist creatively and nonviolently. Disciples of Jesus love their enemies because God does. They learn to be perfect in mercy.

These are concrete discipleship actions by which the disciples live out the Beatitudes and become signal communities of salt, light, and cities on hills—beacons of hope.

Psychologically, Jesus is challenging us to move from the instinctive, fight-or-flight, raw sex part of our animal brain, to the human part of our brain. Using this intelligent, creative thinking, the problem-solving capacity of the human brain can result in better choices. The fruit of this can be de-escalation of conflict through reducing fear and anger, and fostering trust, peacemaking, and cooperation. Game theory, as already mentioned, suggests we are then all better off.[1]

Might there be a possible seventh discipleship commandment?

---

1. Author conversation with James Rathbone.

Six Discipleship Commandments: Some Conclusions

The Sermon on the Mount does not have a focus on ecological crisis and climate change. That was not an issue 2,000 years ago. The possible use of nuclear weapons remains a big issue, but climate change is perhaps the most haunting, biggest issue facing humanity.

The Sermon on the Mount is not intended to be a comprehensive summary of the ethos and spirit of the kingdom, but it is very good at stirring our imagination in new kingdom ways. We also get insight into the mind of Matthew's Jesus and how Jesus is creatively thinking.

Thus, consider this possible seventh discipleship commandment:

Traditional Righteousness	The Vicious Cycle	Transforming Initiative
5:49*—"You have heard that it was said, 'You shall be fruitful and multiply, fill and subdue the earth, and have dominion over all living things.'" [* Versification is to aid discussion. This is a hypothetical passage.]	⁵⁰ But I say to you, the earth that the Father created as very good, now trembles in great agony. Species crafted by living processes over eons of time are being forever lost. ⁵¹ The heat of hell is coming upon the earth, and your children and their children and all of life shall be caught in the whirlwind of your irresponsibility. ⁵² Can you not see the signs of your times? A dreadful day is coming if there is no repentance on the earth.	⁵³ Live simply as I do, walk as I do. You do not own the earth, your loving Father, carpenter of the universe, does. ⁵⁴ Your task is to be trustees of the earth's well-being, accountable to your Creator. ⁵⁵ Therefore, be stewards of care, gardeners of earth's flourishing. Care for the web of life that you are also part of. In its health lies your own well-being. ⁵⁶ Think of the welfare of your children, and their children, for the next seven generations. Pass on the earth in better shape than you received it. ⁵⁷ It is the meek, and those who are organizing as caring stewards, who shall turn back the coming destruction. ⁵⁸ It is those who live as light in the darkness and preach salty repentance, who shall yet save the earth from the judgement that is coming.

Part Two | Sermon on the Mount

REFLECTIONS

1. What are your first responses to this new discipleship commandment?
2. What would you change? How might you edit or improve it?
3. Is it okay to creatively and prayerfully do this kind of exercise? What might be your reservations?
4. Are there other issues you could do a similar exercise with?

Prayer Thought

Help us, Lord Jesus, to be open to the guidance of your Spirit. Help us to understand more clearly our responsibilities as your disciples, and to see fresh truths in the Sermon on the Mount for us today. Amen.

14

Not Showing Off and Authentic Prayer

INTODUCTION

Read the passage:

6 ¹ "Beware of practicing your piety before others in order to be seen by them; for then you have no reward from your Father in heaven. ² So whenever you give alms, do not sound a trumpet before you, as the hypocrites do in the synagogues and in the streets, so that they may be praised by others. Truly I tell you, they have received their reward. ³ But when you give alms, do not let your left hand know what your right hand is doing, ⁴ so that your alms may be done in secret; and your Father who sees in secret will reward you.

⁵ "And whenever you pray, do not be like the hypocrites; for they love to stand and pray in the synagogues and at the street corners, so that they may be seen by others. Truly I tell you, they have received their reward. ⁶ But whenever you pray, go into your room and shut the door and pray to your Father who is in secret; and your Father who sees in secret will reward you.

⁷ "When you are praying, do not heap up empty phrases as the Gentiles do; for they think that they will be heard because of their many words. ⁸ Do not be like them, for your Father knows what you need before you ask him.

⁹ "Pray then in this way:

Our Father in heaven,
> hallowed be your name.
> ¹⁰ Your kingdom come.
> Your will be done,
> > on earth as it is in heaven.
> ¹¹ Give us this day our daily bread.
> ¹² And forgive us our debts,
> > as we also have forgiven our debtors.
> ¹³ And do not bring us to the time of trial,
> > but rescue us from the evil one.

¹⁴ For if you forgive others their trespasses, your heavenly Father will also forgive you; ¹⁵ but if you do not forgive others, neither will your Father forgive your trespasses.

¹⁶ "And whenever you fast, do not look dismal, like the hypocrites, for they disfigure their faces so as to show others that they are fasting. Truly I tell you, they have received their reward. ¹⁷ But when you fast, put oil on your head and wash your face, ¹⁸ so that your fasting may be seen not by others but by your Father who is in secret; and your Father who sees in secret will reward you."

(Matthew 6:1–18)

First Thoughts

1. The spiritual practices of almsgiving, prayer, and fasting are lifted up in this passage. Do you practice these regularly? Are they helpful?

2. How should we do these spiritual practices, according to Jesus? What is the temptation we should seek to avoid? What harm might be done otherwise?

Not Showing Off and Authentic Prayer

Almsgiving, prayer, and fasting are spiritual practices. They are to be done in secret, hidden. In contrast, living the Beatitudes transforms a people to become salt, light, a city on a hill. How the followers of Jesus live and love in community is to become naturally visible as part of their witness of the kingdom life. On the other hand, parading our individual piety is prideful, egotistical, and betrays Christian communal life. It is a form of virtue signaling. Humility is required for authentic community to happen. Christian life is a team, not solo, activity.

Does donating openly and publicly harm the recipient, discredit the giver, and betray Christian love? Famous medieval rabbi and philosopher Maimonides (1138–1204) helpfully distinguishes between eight different levels of giving, from grudging to anonymous. At the anonymous giving level the recipient does not know who has given, and the giver does not know who has received. If they meet, one is not indebted to the other, they are equal in fellowship. The very highest form of giving is enabling someone to be independent, no longer dependent on charity.[1] Jesus is teaching, like Maimonides, a higher form of generosity.

Fasting can express regret for sinning, be for spiritual elevation, and be on special days like Yom Kippur, the Day of Atonement. Fasting can also be in solidarity with the hungry, the poor, and the oppressed. Isaiah says these challenging words:

> Is not this the fast that I choose:
> > to loose the bonds of injustice,
> > to undo the thongs of the yoke,
> to let the oppressed go free,
> > and to break every yoke?
> Is it not to share your bread with the hungry,
> > and bring the homeless poor into your house;
> when you see the naked, to cover them,
> > and not to hide yourself from your own kin?
> Then your light shall break forth like the dawn . . .[2]

Jesus' teachings on almsgiving, authentic prayer, and fasting frame the Lord's Prayer in this passage.

The Lord's Prayer could also be called the Disciple's Prayer, or the Kingdom Prayer. It is placed in the middle of the Sermon on the Mount, fifty-six verses come before, forty-eight verses afterwards. It is the theological

---

1. See, for example, Shuchat, "Eight Degrees of Giving."
2. Isaiah 58:6–8a.

and spiritual heart of the Sermon on the Mount. Let us look carefully at each verse:

> [9] Our Father in heaven,
>   hallowed be your name.

It starts personally. We address God as "Father," as a loving parent. We say "*Our* Father . . ." God is the loving father of *all* of humanity.[3] This prayer begins by including every person. We continue with praise, "hallowed be your name," holy is your name.

> [10] Your kingdom come.
>   Your will be done,
>   on earth as it is in heaven.

Then we pray for God's redemptive, liberating kingdom to come. On earth! Now! God's kingdom comes by our yes to God's way. God's will, as described so far in the Sermon on the Mount, includes reconciling, faithfulness in marriage, consistent truthful talk, not retaliating, and loving enemies.

> [11] Give us this day our daily bread.

God's kingdom includes the necessities for life. It is the end of poverty, hunger, and degradation, as well as enough food, shelter, health care, and clothing for all. This kingdom prayer is concerned about our physical well-being. We pray for "*us*," everyone, to have enough of the necessities of life. We pray in solidarity with others. We pray for exodus for all, economic justice for everyone.

> [12] And forgive us our debts,
>   as we also have forgiven our debtors.

The Lord's Prayer is also about debt forgiveness. The word in Greek translated "debtors" means financial debts. In first-century Judea and Galilee, as in all peasant economies, a family's survival depends on the whole village sharing risk and sharing bounty. Village life in the Galilean corner of the Roman Empire was under great stress because of predatory taxation in an occupied land ruled by client king Herod Antipas. Families were thus much more vulnerable with this exploitative taxation. They borrowed in bad years to feed their families, with their land as security, and if they could not repay their debt, they lost their land. Then they were even more vulnerable. Later in Matthew, Jesus tells the parable of the unforgiving servant,

---

3. Betz and Schweiker, "Concerning Mountains and Morals," 19.

who was forgiven an enormous debt, but promptly threw a fellow servant into prison for not paying a small debt.[4]

The community of Jesus forgive each other their debts, and share risk and bread. This practice of sharing was continued in urban centers also. Luke tells the story in Acts of the early Jerusalem community sharing all things in common.[5] This sharing was almost certainly happening in the Antioch congregation, possibly the first to hear Matthew's Gospel. The practice of economic sharing is not new, but deeply embedded in the Torah, beginning with the story of the exodus, of God freeing slaves in Egypt. This practice of liberating the poor from slavery and debts in Israel continued in the practices of the Sabbath Year and the Year of Jubilee.[6] The Jubilee Year was held every fiftieth year, and included restoring lands sold during the fifty years back to the original owners. In praying these words "And forgive us our debts, as we also have forgiven our debtors," the community of Jesus stands with each other in good and bad economic times.[7]

> [13] And do not bring us to the time of trial,
> but rescue us from the evil one.

We close the Lord's Prayer by asking for protection from the time of trial. In other translations, we pray to be saved from temptation. Since temptation begins with coveting, we are mindful of this weakness in us, and the dangers it can lead us into. Roman occupation and bad harvests were times of trial. We should not be tempted to participate in collaborating with imperial Rome (or its equivalent today) for personal gain.

The Lord's Prayer seeks a very different system on earth than that of the Roman Empire. God as Father is very different to Caesar as Father, as already discussed.[8] We pray to God as Father for the daily necessities of all, for mutual forgiveness of debts, and not to be tempted by coveting. This is what it means for God's upside-down empire to come. The use of "Father" throughout Matthew's Gospel subversively overturns patriarchy and hierarchy.

---

4. Matthew 18:23–35.

5. Acts 2:44–45.

6. For the Sabbatical Year see Deuteronomy 15:1–18. For the Year of Jubilee see Leviticus 25.

7. See Swancutt, "'Forgive Us Our Debts.'"

8. Matthew 5:38–48.

Forgiveness is re-emphasized in the next verse after the Lord's Prayer with these words:

> [14] For if you forgive others their trespasses, your heavenly Father will also forgive you; [15] but if you do not forgive others, neither will your Father forgive your trespasses.

The Lord's Prayer in the NRSV translation speaks of forgiving financial debts (verse 12). Now (verses 14–15) we read about forgiving moral debts (sin). Forgiveness of either has one condition. Having been forgiven, we must forgive others. Jesus returns to this theme of forgiveness later in Matthew's Gospel at chapter 18.[9]

What is an example of this kind of unreserved forgiveness? On October 2, 2006 Charles Carl Roberts entered an Amish one-room schoolhouse in West Nickel Mines, Lancaster County, Pennsylvania, and shot eight of ten girls, killing five of them. Roberts then killed himself. What surprised so many people was the immediate reaching out by members of the Amish community to the Roberts family in compassion and forgiveness. What made the Amish react in this way? The authors of the book *Amish Grace* suggest it was the daily practice of saying the Lord's Prayer at the beginning and end of the day, and as grace silently before meals. This prayer, prayed several times a day, shaped these disciples into the habit and culture of forgiving others.[10] Perhaps there is something to learn from their example.

Finally, what can we say psychologically about this teaching? Humans have survived by working together, cooperating. Humans in solitary confinement go insane. As humans we want to be liked; there is safety in approval—it means inclusion in the group. So, demonstrating generous almsgiving, pious praying, and fasting is one way to seek approval. Except we also do not trust show-offs, or those trying to demonstrate they are better than the rest of us. Such behavior does not lead to authentic, cooperative community.[11]

---

9. Matthew 18:21–35.
10. Kraybill et al., *Amish Grace*, 90–98.
11. Author conversation with James Rathbone.

Not Showing Off and Authentic Prayer

REFLECTIONS

1. Read the Lord's Prayer (Matthew 6:9–13). What do you learn from the structure and content of the Lord's Prayer?
2. The Lord's Prayer is brief. Try writing a brief prayer following the same simple formula of grateful praise and requests for needs. Then share it. Does it make a difference if you use "we, our," and "us," or "me, my," and "I"?
3. What can we learn from how the Amish practice of regularly praying the Lord's Prayer? How might saying the Lord's Prayer consistently help us stand in solidarity with the poor, and in commitment to forgive others, no matter how terrible their sin against us?
4. Have you found fasting helpful as a spiritual practice, and if so, how?
5. In what ways is charitable giving in secret good for our souls, good for community, and good for the recipient?

Prayer Thought

Pray the Lord's Prayer thoughtfully in a daily pattern like the Amish do: when waking, before food, and at the end of the day. Try this for a week. Then review how this practice blesses both you and others. Close now by saying the Lord's Prayer.

15

What Is Your Heart Set On?

INTRODUCTION

Read the passage:

> **6** [19] "Do not store up for yourselves treasures on earth, where moth and rust consume and where thieves break in and steal; [20] but store up for yourselves treasures in heaven, where neither moth nor rust consumes and where thieves do not break in and steal. [21] For where your treasure is, there your heart will be also.
> [22] "The eye is the lamp of the body. So, if your eye is healthy, your whole body will be full of light; [23] but if your eye is unhealthy, your whole body will be full of darkness. If then the light in you is darkness, how great is the darkness!" (Matthew 6:19–23)

First Thoughts

1. What is challenging for you in these teachings?

2. "Do not store up for yourselves treasures on earth, where moth and rust consume and where thieves break in and steal." How would you translate these ideas so they are understandable in your culture today?

There is no peace without economic justice. There are over 3,600 verses in the Bible addressing poverty and justice.[1] As already stated, the big story in the Hebrew Scriptures is that of exodus, the freeing of Hebrew slaves from Egypt. In the burning bush experience Moses heard these words:

> "I have observed the misery of my people who are in Egypt; I have heard their cry on account of their taskmasters. Indeed, I know their sufferings, and I have come down to deliver them from the Egyptians ..."[2]

You cannot be poorer than a slave. Slaves do not own even their own bodies. God seeks passionately to end economic injustice. Economic justice is the continuing cry of other Hebrew prophets like the writers of Isaiah, Jeremiah, and Amos. Hear, for example, the prophetic cry of Amos:

> I hate, I despise your festivals,
>   and I take no delight in your solemn assemblies ...
> Take away from me the noise of your songs;
>   I will not listen to the melody of your harps.
> But let justice roll down like waters,
>   and righteousness like an ever-flowing stream.[3]

As mentioned earlier, every seven years (a sabbath year) slaves were to be freed, debts forgiven, and the land rested.[4] The Jubilee Year or Year of Restoration, every forty-nine years (seven times seven years) was a super sabbath year. Land was redistributed so that a growing gap between rich and poor was prevented.[5] This is the continuation of the spirit of the exodus. In the beginning the earth was created to bless all the human family with enough to spare, and the Hebrew prophets sought this goal again and again.

1. See *Poverty and Justice Bible* (NRSV), Bible Society, 2013.
2. Exodus 3:7–8.
3. Amos 5:21, 23–24.
4. Leviticus 25:1–7; Deuteronomy 15:1–18.
5. Leviticus 25:8–24.

Part Two | Sermon on the Mount

Jesus stood in the exodus/Moses tradition in Luke's Gospel when he read Isaiah 61:1–2a/58:6 at the beginning of his public ministry (Luke 4:18–19), and when he alluded to this same Isaiah passage in the Beatitudes opening the Sermon on the Mount.[6] The night before he was crucified, Jesus shared in the Passover meal, a festival and a party that remembers the exodus and liberation of slaves from Egypt. At that Passover, he added a new remembrance, that of his suffering, that became the Lord's Supper, communion. When the early Christians in Jerusalem held their goods in common, the spirit of the exodus became a communal reality.[7] The monastic tradition continues this tradition of communal discipleship, as do the Hutterites, and the Bruderhof communities. The Bible has a strong, but neglected, tradition of communal socialism.

The gap between the rich and poor today is a scandal. An Oxfam report states the following:

- Since 2020, the beginning of this decade of division, the five richest men in the world have seen their fortunes more than double, while almost five billion people have seen their wealth fall.
- Seven out of ten of the world's biggest corporations have a billionaire CEO or a billionaire as their principal shareholder.
- Globally, men own US$105 trillion more wealth than women—the difference in wealth is equivalent to more than four times the size of the US economy.
- The world's richest 1 percent own 43 percent of all global financial assets.
- The richest 1 percent globally emit as much carbon pollution as the poorest two-thirds of humanity.
- In the US, the wealth of a typical black household is just 15.8 percent of that of a typical white household.[8]

In this passage from the Sermon on the Mount, Jesus is addressing our hearts. He is saying do not set your heart on material things. Do not hoard wealth, do not amass large savings, do not trust in the stock market. Inflation and stock market crashes can take your wealth. Instead, with

---

6. Luke 4:18–19; Matthew 5:3–4, 12.
7. Acts 2:43–45; 4:32–37.
8. Riddell et al., "Inequality Inc.," 5.

compassion, invest now in the needs of the poor. If your heart is filled with compassion for the poor, and your wealth is invested in their well-being, then your heart is in the right place.

If my eyes are focused on acquiring wealth, coveting money, then is my whole soul in darkness? If my eyes are focused with compassion for the poor, then is my whole being filled with light?

Would an alcoholic be put in charge of a wine shop? Would a drug addict be put in charge of a pharmacy? Is possessing great wealth a sign of a serious addiction?

In the kingdom of God we own nothing, God owns everything. We are simply stewards, trustees, managers of God's bounty commissioned to ensure that all are blessed with enough.

We are to be careful what we set our hearts on.

REFLECTIONS

1. Do we try to satisfy our spiritual needs with material things that are limited in a finite world?
2. How does advertising work? Does advertising create false needs and arouse our tendency/weakness to covet? Can you give examples of things you have perhaps been drawn to covet through advertisements?
3. Who do you think should be in charge of the economy? How should the economy be managed so all are blessed?
4. There are different responses to possessions. For instance, steward or owner, stingy or generous. Can you give examples of people who have modeled being generous stewards? What are/were they like as people? What might people say about me?

Prayer Thought

What is my heart really set upon? Help me God to do your will. May I let your Spirit work in my soul and free me from coveting, and relax into gratitude and be content with enough. Amen.

16

Serving Two Masters and Facing Worry

INTRODUCTION

Read the passage:

> **6** [24] "No one can serve two masters; for a slave will either hate the one and love the other, or be devoted to the one and despise the other. You cannot serve God and wealth.
> [25] "Therefore I tell you, do not worry about your life, what you will eat or what you will drink, or about your body, what you will wear. Is not life more than food, and the body more than clothing? [26] Look at the birds of the air; they neither sow nor reap nor gather into barns, and yet your heavenly Father feeds them. Are you not of more value than they? [27] And can any of you by worrying add a single hour to your span of life? [28] And why do you worry about clothing? Consider the lilies of the field, how they grow; they neither toil nor spin, [29] yet I tell you, even Solomon in all his glory was not clothed like one of these. [30] But if God so clothes the grass of the field, which is alive today and tomorrow is thrown into the oven, will he not much more clothe you—you of little faith? [31] Therefore do not worry, saying, 'What will we eat?' or 'What will we drink?' or 'What will we wear?' [32] For it is the Gentiles who strive for all these things; and indeed your heavenly Father knows that you need all these things. [33] But strive first for the kingdom of God and his righteousness, and all these things will be given to you as well.

Serving Two Masters and Facing Worry

[34] "So do not worry about tomorrow, for tomorrow will bring worries of its own. Today's trouble is enough for today."
(Matthew 6:24–34)

First Thoughts

1. What is personally challenging for you in this passage?

2. How do you cope with worry?

A HOLE IN OUR SOUL?

One boss is hard enough. To have two bosses makes a worker's job very difficult. There can be so much stress and tension with each boss wanting all of you. So single-line management, just one boss, is the best way of supervising a worker. Jesus understood the problem of two bosses. We have to choose one: God or wealth.

A person ruthlessly committed to money can discover in the end a life tragically wasted, as well as terribly destructive of those around her or him. Erich Fromm, the noted psychologist, wrote: "Greed is a bottomless pit which exhausts the person in an endless effort to satisfy the need without ever reaching satisfaction."[1]

Is there a hole in our soul that only the Infinite, God's Spirit, can fill and satisfy? I have found helpful Ernst Schumacher's insight about the human condition. He was a German economist who worked in Britain.

---

1. Fromm, *Fear of Freedom*, 100.

Economics deals with the problem of material scarcity. In his book *Small is Beautiful*, Schumacher suggests that to understand the human problem is

> to see the hollowness and fundamental unsatisfactoriness of a life devoted primarily to the pursuit of material ends, to the neglect of the spiritual. Such a life necessarily sets [person] against [person] and nation against nation, *because [a human's] needs are infinite and infinitude can be achieved only in the spiritual realm, never in the material*" (emphasis added).[2]

Our addiction to more and more things impoverishes others and leads to injustice, conflict, and war. Both communism and neoliberal capitalism are equally materialistic. Unlike neoliberal capitalism, communism wants to share goods equally, but in the former Soviet Union, and present-day Cuba and China, power was/is not equally shared.

In an unbalanced life, addiction to power to get more "stuff" is a special concern. "Power tends to corrupt and absolute power corrupts absolutely" said Lord Acton.[3] It is unaccountable power that is corrupting—witness autocrats and the rich.

If Schumacher is right, he helps us understand some of Jesus' sayings, like:

> "You cannot serve God and wealth";
> "One does not live by bread alone";
> "Those who drink of the water that I will give them will never be thirsty."[4]

To seek to satisfy our deepest spiritual yearnings—the hole in our soul—by accumulating more and more stuff is a colossal human mistake. It damages ourselves, others, and the earth in a heartless addiction and scramble for things. And it leaves us still wanting, still unsatisfied, deeply troubled.[5]

What might be a psychologist's commentary on Matthew 6:19–34? Rathbone states first of all that psychologically, humans are generally poor at predicting future satisfaction. For instance, research shows that the lift from winning the lottery wears off after about six months. If material things do not bring deep satisfaction, what does? It is relationships, Rathbone

---

2. Schumacher, *Small is Beautiful*, 38.
3. Acton, "Letter to Archbishop Mandell Creighton."
4. Matthew 6:24; 4:4; John 4:14.
5. For this insight see Schumacher, *Small Is Beautiful*, 38.

states. What is so good about relationships? Rathbone summarizes as follows:

- Relationships are the best predictor of long-term health.
- Social connections improve happiness, physical health, and longevity; loneliness kills.
- Securely attached relationships protect our mental ability to know, learn, and understand, as well as our physical health.
- Quality not quantity of relationships is the key. A circle of close friends who you see regularly and do things with is much more important than masses of Facebook friends.[6]

In addition, serving a cause bigger than ourselves brings meaning and purpose. Interestingly, this is how Jesus ends this Sermon on the Mount passage: "Strive first for the kingdom of God and his righteousness and all these things will be given to you as well."[7] Serving the kingdom of God and God's justice, contributing to better communities, can be deeply meaningful.

Two British epidemiologists, Richard Wilkinson and Kate Pickett, have comprehensively studied the effects of income inequality on human and societal well-being. The greater the gap between rich and poor in a society the lower life expectancy, and the higher infant mortality, mental illness, illicit drug use, obesity, violence, and imprisonment rates. There is also less trust, and community life is weakened. Unequal societies are dysfunctional. Examples of unequal societies include the US and the UK. Countries like Japan and Scandinavian nations are more equal and healthier, children do better, there are lower teenage birthrates and higher social mobility.[8] Astonishingly, 95 percent of human existence for the last 200,000–250,000 years has been in egalitarian hunter/gatherer societies. Only since the development of agriculture, and reinforced later by the industrial revolution, has the pyramid of inequality arisen.[9] Is Jesus calling us back to *normal* human equality?

---

6. Rathbone, "Happily Ever After." With permission I have simplified for ease of understanding.

7. Matthew 6:31.

8. Wilkinson and Pickett, *Inner Level*, xvii

9. Wilkinson and Pickett, *Inner Level*, 120–22.

To return to the Torah and the Prophets, idolatry is to worship a thing instead of God. When we worship God we also value every person, since we are all made in the image of God. To worship money is idolatry and ends up destroying the personal, the relational, the worth of every human.

Thus, Jesus says "Do not worry!" Celebrate life, today's gift of existence! Consider the birds of the air and the lilies of the field. They do not worry, nor strive, nor hoard. They are not anxious about how they look, nor the latest fashions, yet God provides for them and makes them beautiful. How much more are you loved and valued by God. It is in God's love that we discover our real worth and find peace for our restless, agitated soul.

Finally, in chapter 6, Matthew's Jesus is addressing the heart of the human condition. We worry about our image, we worry about not having enough, we worry when we compare ourselves to those better off than ourselves, we worry about the future. We seek satisfaction and meaning in wealth and things, instead of loving relationships and authentic community. Competition for more and more stuff leads to violence, and a consumerism that is creating a massive climate crisis, and still does not satisfy our souls or quench our anxieties. In asking for us to be delivered from the evil one in the Lord's Prayer, we are praying for deliverance from economic, religious, and violent temptations as we seek to satisfy our demanding, worried, anxious egos.

A little later in Matthew, Jesus invites us with these words of promise and assurance: "Come to me, all you that are weary and are carrying heavy burdens, and I will give you rest."[10]

REFLECTIONS

1. To what extent are you anxious about having enough? What do you worry about on a daily basis? What are you anxious about today?

2. Economics has been called the dismal science, the science of scarcity. Is Jesus talking here about the opposite, a theology of abundance? That there is enough for everyone if we share? Do you see the world through the lens of scarcity or abundance?

3. What happens when we panic-buy and hoard? How have you been affected?

---

10. Matthew 11:28.

4. The "parable" of the ant and the grasshopper is a children's story about ants who work during the summer to store food for winter, and the grasshopper who spends the summer singing and dancing, but then starves when winter comes. Can we prudently plan for the future, without it becoming obsessive, an addiction to hoarding?

5. "Do not seek for physical riches, but riches of the heart. Seek love, not money. Love is forever, everything else is not."[11] What do you think?

6. What does it mean for you to seek God's kingdom first each day? What does it mean to strive for God's kingdom?

Prayer Thought

Calm my fears, God of Peace. Center my heart in your loving presence. Fill me with your love so that there is no need for worry. May both the Spirit and words of Jesus lead me in the paths of righteousness for your name's sake. Amen.

---

11. Agneta, a reader of an earlier draft of this book, suggested this.

17

Judging Others

INTRODUCTION

Read the passage:

> 7 ¹ "Do not judge, so that you may not be judged. ² For with the judgment you make you will be judged, and the measure you give will be the measure you get. ³ Why do you see the speck in your neighbor's eye, but do not notice the log in your own eye? ⁴ Or how can you say to your neighbor, 'Let me take the speck out of your eye,' while the log is in your own eye? ⁵ You hypocrite, first take the log out of your own eye, and then you will see clearly to take the speck out of your neighbor's eye.
>
> ⁶ "Do not give what is holy to dogs; and do not throw your pearls before swine, or they will trample them under foot and turn and maul you." (Matthew 7:1–6)

First Thoughts

1. What is Jesus teaching here? Is there anything that puzzles you?

2. How might having a judgemental attitude be a problem when relating with others?

NOT JUDGING BUT ALSO NOT THROWING PEARLS BEFORE PIGS

"Do not judge, so you may not be judged!" Judgement here sounds more like condemnation. The message could perhaps be restated: "Do not condemn others so you are not condemned."

Judging others may be a way of relieving, for a moment, my own guilt by arguing that another person is more guilty than I am, worse than me. Or I may be projecting my guilt on another, and then unjustly judging them for my hidden sins. Either way, for a little while, I do not feel quite so bad, but the problem of unrelieved guilt still lurks and gnaws in my soul.

Psychologically, judging others is complex. We compare ourselves for a good reason—we do not want to be rejected. However, if we feel we are not keeping up, then in our insecurity we can work to bring others down. Children who find school challenging may bully a clever child. A judgemental attitude can say a lot about the person making the judgement. Empathy and compassion are an alternative way. For instance, a child abuser may have been abused. I may judge others because I have been judged. It is good to look at oneself, understand our own story, then exercise grace to ourselves and others.[1]

Paul wrote, "All have sinned and fall short of the glory of God" (Romans 3:23). We are all sinners, and when I realize this is true for me, I find I cannot throw the first stone. Guilt is a soul problem. Healthy guilt is like the oil warning light on a car dashboard. When the flashing oil light comes on it tells me there is a problem. I can then do something before it is too late. When I acknowledge my own real guilt (with embarrassment, painfully, reluctantly), I can find the good news of Christ is really true. I can find full and complete forgiveness. Christ's generous, merciful forgiveness is the real

---

1. Author conversation with James Rathbone.

cure for my soul problem of guilt. I delight and revel in the reality that God truly grants me an ever fresh and new beginning. Time after time. My hero is the apostle Peter, always making mistakes, always being forgiven, always risking again in faith, always loved by Jesus.

God does speak in judgement. That is the prophetic tradition of Israel. Moses, Nathan, Isaiah, Amos, and John the Baptist spoke in judgement against those who broke the Ten Commandments, and against those who did not help and protect the poor, the stranger, the widow, and the orphaned. However, God's judgement is both righteous and *redemptive*. In divine judgement God is seeking to save us from our sins. We worship a redemptive God, who like the father of the prodigal child is looking out for us, yearning for us, while we are yet a long way off (Luke 15:19–24).

Neither can we divide the world simply into good people and bad people, and then destroy the bad. As the Russian author Aleksandr Solzhenitsyn said, "The line dividing good and evil cuts through the heart of every human being. And who is willing to destroy a piece of his own heart?"[2] Martin Luther King Jr. said something similar: "There is some good in the worst of us and some evil in the best of us. When we discover this, we are less prone to hate our enemies."[3] One could add, and then it is also more difficult to do violence against them, for "who is willing to destroy a piece of his own heart"?

Two friends, Karen and Lisa, would tease each other, "Confess your own sins! Not mine!" They were saying, "Don't tell my sins to the world, tell your own!" I should not be quick to judge others when there is a massive log in my own eye!

Gossip is a kind of judging. It is sneaky, behind a person's back. The accused is judged when she or he is not able to defend themselves. According to Matthew 18, our first step is to deal directly with the other person who has upset us. And we do so with love and ready forgiveness.[4] Gossip is a betrayal of a sister or brother, and damages community. The Bruderhof community practices Matthew 18 really well.

Prejudice is pre-judging. We judge an individual because she or he belongs to a particular group—black or white, Jewish or Muslim, male or female, rich or poor. This is stereotyping and is neither just nor accurate.

---

2. Solzhenitsyn, *Gulag Archipelago*.
3. King, *Strength to Love*, 49.
4. Matthew 18:15–17.

Judging Others

The distinction that comes from belonging to a group is abolished through baptism, said Paul in Galatians:

> As many of you as were baptized into Christ have clothed yourselves with Christ. There is no longer Jew or Greek, there is no longer slave or free, there is no longer male and female; for all of you are one in Christ Jesus.[5]

Great evil and horrendous violence has been done through prejudice or stereotyping, including racism, war, and genocide.

"Do not give what is holy to dogs; and do not throw pearls before swine"—what does this mean?[6] This difficult verse sounds judgmental, even contradictory to the first five verses of this chapter. Perhaps one interpretation is that discernment or wisdom is needed in choosing with whom to share the gospel. There are some who will be so antagonized that it is better, at least for the time being, to leave them alone. We should avoid insensitively provoking antagonism and enmity with our message. The witness of our lives, however, can still continue until such a time that a person is open and ready for us to share more.

In summary, do not judge. That is a violence. It is only God's place to judge, and God is merciful. When we judge and dismiss another, we do not see what they have suffered. We have not walked in their shoes. If we understood another person's story, this perhaps would evoke compassion and understanding rather than condemnation. In judging others, we are blind twice: blind to our own sin and blind to the grace that is equally available for the people we have judged. However, we also should be discerning. Be wise with whom you seek to share the gospel. Some people are not ready now, but may be open at another time. So do not provoke them, but continue quietly and humbly to live the life of a disciple of Jesus.

REFLECTIONS

1. What do you tend to be judgemental about?
2. Is harsh judgement of others the result of unresolved guilt in my own soul? What are your thoughts about this question?
3. How might condemning judgement be unjust and lead to violence?

5. Galatians 3:27–28.
6. Matthew 7:6.

4. Is gossip also a form of judgement? How does gossip damage Christian fellowship and other communities that we are part of?

5. How might discernment about the right time to share something about Christ be different from harsh judgement?

Prayer Thought

Loving God, you know my heart, the burdens I carry from the mistakes I have made. Heal me now of my guilt, help me to be wiser and make better decisions. Enable me with empathy and insight to love others rather than condemn them. Help me to discern the right time to share your love with others. Amen.

18

Ask, Search, Knock!

INTRODUCTION

Read the passage:

> 7 ⁷ "Ask, and it will be given you; search, and you will find; knock, and the door will be opened for you. ⁸ For everyone who asks receives, and everyone who searches finds, and for everyone who knocks, the door will be opened. ⁹ Is there anyone among you who, if your child asks for bread, will give a stone? ¹⁰ Or if the child asks for a fish, will give a snake? ¹¹ If you then, who are evil, know how to give good gifts to your children, how much more will your Father in heaven give good things to those who ask him!" (Matthew 7:7–11)

> "If you then, who are evil, know how to give good gifts to your children, how much more will the heavenly Father give the Holy Spirit to those who ask him!" (Luke 11:13)

> "If any of you is lacking in wisdom, ask God, who gives to all generously and ungrudgingly, and it will be given you." (James 1:5)

First Thoughts

1. When have you been a seeker after God and for a better understanding of God's ways? How were you blessed by your prayerful seeking?

2. "Ask, search, knock." How might this be a wonderful invitation to not only you, but something you can share with others? What are your thoughts about this?

CONFIDENT PRAYER AND REAL ANSWERS?

Ask, search, knock! God promises to respond! Our faith is an experiential faith. God is not a theory, but a loving reality who is approachable and longs for relationship with us. The Divine wants you and me to come into relationship. The Divine answers prayers with good gifts. According to Luke's version of this passage, the Holy Spirit is the greatest gift that our loving heavenly Parent wants to grant us. Wisdom, guidance is another good gift, according to the Letter of James[1]—which has some other significant parallels with the Sermon on the Mount.[2] To live out the Sermon on the Mount, we need both wisdom and power. We need to pray for help. We cannot live this way in our own strength. We need grace. The earliest disciples testified that the God of Jesus was approachable, like a loving mother or father, like Jesus was. This can be our testimony also.

Does religious experience really happen in our secular times? David Hay, a zoologist in the UK, became interested in studying religious experience through his teacher, a former professor of zoology at Oxford, Sir Alister Hardy. After his retirement, Hardy set up the Religious Experience Research Unit, which used modern social surveying techniques in the study of religious experience. When I taught at Westminster College, Oxford, the Alister Hardy Religious Experience Research Unit was based there, and I was friends with the directors. David Hay's research found that many people in secular Britain reported religious experiences. So, while few may go to church, many have had a sense of spiritual reality. However, in a secular culture people are shy about talking about such experiences, and do not find each other easily. Nevertheless, religious experiences are numerous

---

1. James 1:5.
2. See Kirby, "Sermon on the Mount Site."

and impact how people are and act. Research indicates that people with such experiences have a higher sense of well-being and personal integration. In other words, they are mentally healthier. Secondly, as a group, they are more interested in social justice.[3]

So, followers of Jesus can be open to experience, to surprise, to new discoveries about the Divine.

Let me share the story of my friend Peter (not his real name). He lives in China and we met many times over nine years. We are still in contact today. He came from a committed Chinese Communist family. He did his first degree in Marxism, and became a member of the Communist Party while still a student. He then began a master's degree in religious studies—he wanted to trash Christianity convincingly. As part of the master's degree he sometimes met with foreign academics, but did not know they were Christians. In talking with them he was only interested in practicing English, but he liked how friendly they were. The following is Peter's experience of "Asking, seeking, knocking."

> In my studies, I found there were many foolish teachings in the Bible, especially those by Jesus or about Jesus. I was able to make a long list of foolish things found in the Bible or Christian teachings as my studies went further. I remember in a particular Bible group meeting reading these verses, "Ask and it will be given to you, search and you will find, knock and the door will be opened for you," I couldn't help mocking this idea in the study. It seemed so ridiculous! Are you kidding? Will you get whatever you want? How could that be possible? How foolish this statement is! No wonder they say that Christians are simply foolish people, I told myself.
>
> But I was also curious about it. How can someone believe in such ridiculous teachings? Actually, perhaps this was a good opportunity to criticize Jesus and prove his foolishness. It seemed easy to do. What I needed to do was to say a prayer, to ask for something, and see what would happen. Why not try a prayer, I asked myself? This would be like an experiment, and I was a rational, scientific Marxist after all.
>
> So that night I knelt on my bed, rather than the floor, because it was more comfortable. I closed my eyes, it was so easy, anyone can do this I thought. Then I felt I should say something to make it more like acting out a prayer. Unbelievably, however, immediately as I knelt and closed my eyes, I could not say anything, but found

3. Hay, *Exploring Inner Space*, 168–75.

> myself in tears and sobbing already. I was lost in emotion and totally forgot what I was supposed to do. I could not say anything, I didn't know why, no reason, I was just sobbing, sobbing, and sobbing, until I went into a dream, a dream as a vision, a vision as in a dream, that was unspeakably beautiful, but very strange. It is simply impossible for me to be able to describe it, even if I described it in Chinese!
>
> I remember later that night when I awoke and tried to write down that dream, that vision, I could not write anything more than the date. Tears came and I began sobbing again as I was trying to write it down. Later, when reading my diary, I saw only the English text "June 4th, 1998, the date of my rebirth." It was interesting that this vision was not clearly about Jesus or a Christian God, but a vision of a spiritual Being sustaining our world. It was quite in contrast to what I rigidly believed before, that the universe was only material in nature. I clearly knew I was encountering a higher power. My "prayer," done without clearly knowing what to ask, to search for, or at which door to knock, got a sufficient answer, sufficient enough at that time to call it my rebirth that initiated a new journey in my life!
>
> Since that date, many stories have taken place in my life's journey that testifies to how wonderfully the Holy Spirit is working. But at that moment, the testimony was that this encounter was my first realization of the Holy Spirit's work. A later key point is that actually the Holy Spirit had been in working in my life a long time before that realization, so quietly, so gently, so carefully, and most important to me, so p-a-t-i-e-n-t-l-y!
>
> In our lives, may we all be able to pause, and listen, and feel, and commune with God's presence! Amen.

Peter's story is meaningful to me because when I was a young adult I had a similar, totally unexpected experience about three months after my baptism. At the time I was doing a PhD in plant genetics. That spiritual experience was the most profoundly real experience in those three years. I discovered God lovingly welcomes those who ask, seek, knock. But this is not a one-way relationship. God also comes asking for us . . . by name, seeking, searching for our presence. God comes knocking on the door of our heart. God calls us to follow Jesus Christ as disciples in the kingdom mission of peace-giving, justice-making. Then we really need God's help and gifts!

REFLECTIONS

1. What do you think of Peter's experience? Do these kinds of encounters really happen?
2. When did you last ask a parent or someone close to you for help when you really needed it? What happened? Does this help us understand this passage of Scripture?
3. When have you felt God's Spirit near? Has it been small nudges, a sense of joy, being in a presence of love, a sense of connection, or something else?
4. Peter had an amazing experience. Some faithful Christians may not be blessed with such spectacular answers to prayer. What does God's seeming silence mean? Do you have any suggestions to help a person in this situation? Do God's answers come in God's time? Is that why we need to be persistent in asking, and patient in waiting?
5. What big or little questions do you have that would be helped by God's answers?

PRAYER THOUGHT

Loving Parent, in trepidation and uncertainty, but growing trust, I come into your presence to ask you . . . Amen.

19

The Golden Rule—A Basis for a Global Ethic?

INTRODUCTION

Read the passage:

> "In everything do to others as you would have them do to you; for this is the law and the prophets." (Matthew 7:12)

First Thoughts

1. Is this passage a helpful summary of the Sermon on the Mount as well as "the law and the prophets"?

2. Can you think of examples of "do to others as you would have them do to you"?

The Golden Rule—A Basis for a Global Ethic?

CAN WE WORK OUT AN ETHIC FOR ALL?

In half a sentence, Jesus summarizes not only the Sermon on the Mount, but also the heart of the Hebrew Bible. Sometimes this summary is called the Golden Rule. It is another way of saying "Love your neighbor as yourself," which Jesus quoted later in Matthew's Gospel.[1] The Golden Rule is the climax, the capstone, of the Sermon on the Mount.[2]

So, if I do not want to be robbed, I should not steal from others. If I need forgiveness, I should readily forgive. If I do not want people gossiping about me, then I should not gossip about others.

The Golden Rule summarizes the Sermon on the Mount, but also enables us to continue in the spirit of the Sermon on the Mount in working out what we should do in new situations. It gives us a method for discerning what is the loving thing to do.

The Golden Rule is a universal ethic for all people. It is common to all major world religions and many ethical systems. Here is a sample:

> **Hinduism**
> One should never do that to another which one regards as injurious to one's own self.
> (Brihaspati, Mahabharata 13.113.8)
>
> **Buddhism**
> Hurt not others in ways that you yourself would find hurtful.
> In everything do to others as you would have them do to you.
> (Udanavarga 5:18)
>
> **Jainism**
> In happiness and suffering, in joy and grief, we should regard all creatures as we regard our own self.
> (Lord Mahavira, 24th Tirthankara)
>
> **Sikhism**
> Precious like jewels are the minds of all. To hurt them is not at all good. If thou desirest thy Beloved, then hurt thou not anyone's heart.
> (Guru Arjan Dev Ji 259, Guru Granth Sahib)

---

1. Matthew 22:36–40.
2. Hagner, "Ethics and the Sermon," 50.

Part Two | Sermon on the Mount

Judaism
What is hateful to you, do not do to your fellow: this is the whole Torah; the rest is the explanation; go and learn.
(Hillel the Elder, Babylonian Talmud)

Christianity
In everything do to others as you would have them do to you.
(Jesus—Sermon on the Mount—Matthew 7:12)

Islam
As you would have people do to you, do to them; and what you dislike to be done to you, don't do to them.
(A Hadith, Kitab al-Kafi, Volume 2, Book 1, Chapter 66:10)

Baha'i
And if thine eyes be turned towards justice, choose thou for thy neighbour that which thou choosest for thyself.
(*Bahá'u'lláh*)[3]

Humanism
Treat other people as you'd want to be treated in their situation.[4]

The Golden Rule appears to be a universal insight. Is it possible to find other universal insights that can be agreed upon by most, if not all religious and other ethical people?

The first photographs of Earth from space helped us to see clearly that we live on one beautifully made planet, without the distinctions of racial, national, and political boundaries. Mass communications and transport have made the whole planet a neighborhood. Many of our problems now are global problems that require global solutions. Climate change, poverty, war, refugees, and disease epidemics are some of the many issues that require global solutions and international collaboration. Can we have an inspiring global ethic acceptable for all people of good will, whether religious or not? Can we have such a global ethic to help form a basis for international action?

The answer is that a start has been made on a global ethic. In 1893, the first World Parliament of Religions was held in Chicago. About 4,000 people attended from around the world. In 1993, a hundred years later,

---

3. For this and the list above see Wikipedia, "Golden Rule." See also Rodger, *Developing Moral Community*, 14.

4. Understanding Humanism, "Golden Rule."

The Golden Rule—A Basis for a Global Ethic?

the second World Parliament of Religions was held, again in Chicago. Around 6,500 people attended, from every possible religion. At the end of the World Parliament, a declaration toward a global ethic was made. Hans Küng, a Swiss Catholic theologian, wrote an outline global ethic in consultation with many people from other faiths. Küng wrote:

> A global ethic seeks to work out what is already common to the religions of the world now despite all their differences over human conduct, moral values and basic moral convictions. In other words, a global ethic does not reduce the religions to an ethical minimalism but represents the minimum of what the religions of the world already have in common now in the ethical sphere.[5]

Besides the Golden Rule, what else did the 1993 World Parliament of Religions think all religions had in common globally? The 1993 declaration can be summarized as follows:

I. No new global order without a new global ethic.

II. A fundamental demand: Every human being must be treated humanely.

III. Four irrevocable directives:

    1. Commitment to a culture of nonviolence and respect for life.

    2. Commitment to a culture of solidarity and a just economic order.

    3. Commitment to a culture of tolerance and life of truthfulness.

    4. Commitment to a culture of equal rights and partnership between men and women.

IV. A transformation of consciousness.[6]

This was a beginning of a conversation about a global ethic in the World Parliament of Religions, which now meets regularly every few years. Another global ethic is the United Nations Universal Declaration of Human Rights, developed after the atrocities of World War II. This is a secular global ethic, a declaration—not a revelation. It asserts that all humans have certain rights that they are born with, and cannot be sold, bought, or taken away.

---

5. Küng and Kuschel, *Global Ethic*, 7–8.
6. Küng and Kuschel, *Global Ethic*, 7–8.

There are different frameworks for ethics: family, tribal, sectarian, national, or global. The Mafia have one form of a family ethic. In Apartheid South Africa, whites had a tribal ethic which privileged those of European descent, and oppressed black Africans. In Northern Ireland, Catholic and Protestant sectarian ethics were at play in the violent Troubles.

Was European Christendom a kind of tribal ethic in the Crusades and in colonization by European powers, Catholic or Protestant? What about white Christian nationalism today in the US and elsewhere? Is this also a kind of tribal ethic?

The Sermon on the Mount is a global ethic, because it is concerned about the equal well-being of all humans, no matter what family, tribe, faith, or country a person comes from. This is why this teaching of Jesus is so important in our day, and why many, including Mahatma Gandhi, have been inspired by it. Again, the Sermon on the Mount can be summarized in these few words: "In everything do to others as you would have them do to you."

REFLECTIONS

1. How does a tribal or national ethic differ from a global ethic?
2. Can you think of people in history, or that you know personally, who have had either a tribal, national ethic or a global, universal ethic? Who did they love or care for? What were the fruits of their lives?
3. "For God so loved the world . . ." "Go therefore and make disciples of all nations . . ." Are Christians called to have a global/international consciousness? Are we called to live a global ethic? How is the Sermon on the Mount a global ethic?
4. "In everything do to others as you would have them do to you . . ." What does this mean in your simple decisions about others today?

Prayer Thought

"Draw the circle wider . . ." Help me, loving God, to exclude no one from my love who comes across my path today, and in the days ahead. Amen.

20

Decision!

INTRODUCTION

Read the passage:

7 [13] "Enter through the narrow gate; for the gate is wide and the road is easy that leads to destruction, and there are many who take it. [14] For the gate is narrow and the road is hard that leads to life, and there are few who find it.

[15] "Beware of false prophets, who come to you in sheep's clothing but inwardly are ravenous wolves. [16] You will know them by their fruits. Are grapes gathered from thorns, or figs from thistles? [17] In the same way, every good tree bears good fruit, but the bad tree bears bad fruit. [18] A good tree cannot bear bad fruit, nor can a bad tree bear good fruit. [19] Every tree that does not bear good fruit is cut down and thrown into the fire. [20] Thus you will know them by their fruits.

[21] "Not everyone who says to me, 'Lord, Lord,' will enter the kingdom of heaven, but only the one who does the will of my Father in heaven. [22] On that day many will say to me, 'Lord, Lord, did we not prophesy in your name, and cast out demons in your name, and do many deeds of power in your name?' [23] Then I will declare to them, 'I never knew you; go away from me, you evildoers.'

[24] "Everyone then who hears these words of mine and acts on them will be like a wise man who built his house on rock. [25] The rain fell, the floods came, and the winds blew and beat on that house, but it did not fall, because it had been founded on rock. [26] And everyone who hears these words of mine and does not act on them will be like a foolish man who built his house on sand. [27] The rain

fell, and the floods came, and the winds blew and beat against that house, and it fell—and great was its fall!" (Matthew 7:13–27)

First Thoughts

1. What is this passage saying?

2. Is this end passage of the sermon calling for decision on your part? How does the Sermon on the Mount challenge you? What draws you to commitment, and what makes you hesitate?

FACING DECISION

This is a challenging end to the Sermon on the Mount. Reread the above passage. How would you personally summarize the choices that Jesus has put before us? Most of the Sermon on the Mount is made up of sayings, teachings. This ending is the most sermonic part of the Sermon on the Mount. Matthew's Jesus is a preacher here, pushing for decision. As the new Moses, he is asking, will you stay in Egypt, or follow him to the promised land of the upside-down kingdom of God on earth, as it is in heaven?

What makes for a foundation of rock for our discipleship? Let us review the whole Sermon on the Mount briefly.

> Listen to the words of Jesus. Follow the path of the Beatitudes with others. In community, become salt, light, a city on a hill. Be anchored in the Old Testament stories of a good creation, with everyone made in the image of God, the liberating story of the exodus, the prophetic hope of swords into plowshares, and

prophetic concern for the stranger, the widow, the fatherless, and the poor. Revisit some the Ten Commandments, hearing Rabbi Jesus say "but I say to you . . ." Deal with your anger before it is too late, and confront your lust before you commit adultery. Be faithful to your spouse. Be honest in speech, consistently truthful in your words. Turn the other cheek, walk the second mile, creatively resist injustice without retaliation. Love your enemies. Give, pray, and fast sincerely and in secret. Say the Lord's Prayer thoughtfully, regularly. Resist the temptation to pursue wealth. Do not worry about the necessities of life, instead seek first the kingdom of God, its righteousness, and trust that the necessities of life will then be given to you. Secure in God's loving provision, give generously to those in need. Do not judge, prejudge or condemn, but discern wisely and with grace. Ask, seek, knock, knowing God is a loving God with gifts of strength and wisdom to help you along the way if you just ask and try. Practice the Golden Rule, and use it as a bridge with those of other faiths. Jesus respects your choice; it is you who must decide whether or not to choose this kingdom way to live. Following these teachings is to have a solid foundation rock for your discipleship.

There are temptations that pull us along broad, easy ways, to hearken to smooth-talking preachers, to carelessly build on sand rather than rock. There are those who advocate for the violent road, those who pretend to have a peace message, but are wolves. Who are authentic voices of nonviolent justice living? Are we listening to the still, small, voice that calls us along Jesus' narrow path?

Jesus is challenging us to recognize that we have choice. It is through committed action that we can end up where we really want to be. We can then persist through difficulties, recognize misleading voices, and deal with hooks that would drag us off course. James Rathbone says that 90 percent of his work as a psychologist is helping people recognize and become more aware of their hooks, finding effective ways to unhook, and live just and meaningful lives.[1]

Decision! Decision! Decision! Do I choose this Sermon on the Mount way or not?

---

1. Author conversation with James Rathbone.

Part Two | Sermon on the Mount

REFLECTIONS

1. An invitation to hike the narrow way, the temptation to drive the easy way. What do these two routes mean practically for you?

2. How do you know who to believe? Who do you let guide or teach you? How will you know they are authentic? Does the life of Jesus bear good fruit?

3. Martin Buber (1878–1965) was an Austrian Jewish existentialist. He was nominated seven times for the Nobel Peace Prize. For an existentialist, making authentic decisions is what makes us really human. To not decide, to go with the herd, is to abdicate being human. Buber was writing in totalitarian times of world wars, Nazism, and Stalinism. He argued that not deciding is sin.[2] To what extent do you think not deciding, just going with the flow, is dangerous to authentic human living? How might this apply in deciding whether or not to live the Sermon on the Mount?

4. Eberhard Arnold (1883–1935) was a founder of the Bruderhof Christian community in Germany in 1920. He said this about decision for following Christ: "Only the whole Christ for the whole of our life transforms and renews everything. Half of Jesus for half of our life is a lie and a delusion."[3] What do you think of Arnold's challenge? Is he also an existentialist?

5. What are some of the "hooks" that can drag you off the course of living a genuine Christian life?

Prayer Thought

Loving Parent, help me decide now to live this teaching of Jesus wholeheartedly, in your grace, with the gentle, persistent power of the Holy Spirit. Help me each day to build my life on the rock of these teachings, so that when storms come, my discipleship stands. Amen.

2. Cited in Friedman, *Martin Buber*, 33.
3. Arnold, *Inner Life*, 38.

21

After Words

Authority and Healing

INTRODUCTION

Read the passage:

> 7^{28} "Now when Jesus had finished saying these things, the crowds were astounded at his teaching, ^{29} for he taught them as one having authority, and not as their scribes.
> 8^1 When Jesus had come down from the mountain, great crowds followed him."
> (Matthew 7:28–8:1)

> 28^{16} "Now the eleven disciples went to Galilee, to the mountain to which Jesus had directed them. ^{17} When they saw him, they worshiped him; but some doubted. ^{18} And Jesus came and said to them, "All authority in heaven and on earth has been given to me. ^{19} Go therefore and make disciples of all nations, baptizing them in the name of the Father and of the Son and of the Holy Spirit, ^{20} and teaching them to obey everything that I have commanded you. And remember, I am with you always, to the end of the age."
> (Matthew 28:16–20)

Who is Jesus that he can invite us to follow him?

The crowd senses Jesus' authority. They are astounded at his teaching. Jesus in person is authentic and believable for them. I have met people who command my great respect as disciples. Such people have a presence of love, intelligence, kindness, and deep clarity. Their words make sense, offer a better way, and give hope. Their lives show the fruits of the Spirit, and frank confession and repentance when they fail.

If Jesus' authority is first of all personal, then his words make sense. Jesus has authority as a teacher who is for us. The word *authority* is used a further three times in Matthew's Gospel. Jesus has authority to forgive sins.[1] Jesus' authority is questioned by the chief priests and the elders for clearing the temple of cheating animal sellers and money changers, and then for teaching there.[2] Finally, Jesus announces that he has all authority in heaven and earth as he sends out the first apostles to baptize and teach all his commandments in all nations.

Reading Matthew's Gospel as a whole helps expand our understanding of who Jesus really is. Matthew declares right at the beginning that Jesus is of a royal line, from the family of King David. He is the Messiah, God's expected King. Jesus is also more: Emmanuel, "God is with us."[3] In the middle of Matthew's account, Jesus asked the disciples, "Who do you say that I am?" Simon Peter, in a moment of insight, blurts out, "You are the Messiah, the Son of the living God."[4] Six days later in the transfiguration story, Peter, James, and John see Jesus in glory, with Moses on one side, and Elijah on the other. Then a cloud overshadows them, and they hear a terrifying voice saying, "This is my Son, the Beloved; with him I am well pleased; listen to him!" They are overcome with fear, and afterwards Jesus touches them with reassurance, and they see only Jesus.[5] Matthew describes the disciples' growing, expanding awareness of who Jesus is. Likewise, our awareness can also increase. Jesus is more than we first think.

Having taught the Sermon on the Mount, Jesus continues his healing ministry in Galilee. Jesus straightaway demonstrates committed action. The first healing is a leper—the most excluded is now whole and included. The second is poignantly the servant of a Roman centurion. The centurion is praised for his great faith. This story shows that even a Roman officer of the hated occupying army can potentially change sides and serve the empire of

---

1. Matthew 9:2–8.
2. Matthew 21:12–16, 23–27.
3. Matthew 1:18, 23.
4. Matthew 16:15–16.
5. Matthew 17:5–8.

God.[6] Jesus, like Gandhi and others later, distinguishes here between persons and systems. Evil systems that dehumanize and exploit people can be vigorously challenged, resisted, and ultimately dismantled. People in these systems, despite participating in evil, are always to be treated with dignity. Love the sinner, hate the sinful system.

Soon, Jesus calls Matthew the tax collector; another participant in the evil system of Roman exploitation changes sides.[7] Jesus continues to teach and coach the disciples, proclaiming the good news of the kingdom of God. He is concerned about the crowds; they are like sheep without a shepherd. He says to his disciples, "The harvest is plentiful, but the laborers are few; therefore ask the Lord of the harvest to send out laborers into his harvest."[8]

Seeing this huge pastoral need, it is now that Jesus calls together his twelve disciples for their first mission.[9] In sending them out he gives them authority to cast out unclean spirits, and cure every disease and sickness. They are sent first only to the lost sheep of Israel, proclaiming the good news of the kingdom of God and its nearness. They are not to seek payment, nor take a credit card, but to trust that their needs will be met by the people they serve. As they enter homes, they bring peace, and if their peace is not accepted, they depart in peace. They are sent without even a staff as a defensive weapon; they go as sheep in the midst of wolves. They are to be wise and innocent, but are not to be naive; they are in a dangerous world of wolves. They are nonviolent ambassadors of God's kingdom, with a message of *shalom*/peace, now prepared to pass on the teaching of the Sermon on the Mount. They are equipped with healing power to announce the good news of God's coming kingdom in the midst of the bad news of Herod's kingdom, Caesar's empire, and persecution. Jesus instructs them: they should not fear.[10]

God's kingdom is both good news and judgement. There is ultimately accountability. Judgement is also good news because poverty, oppression, violence, and genocide are coming to an end. A day of reckoning is coming, of final judgement. Martin Luther King Jr. said: "The arc of the moral universe is long but it bends toward justice."[11]

6. Matthew 8:5–13.
7. Matthew 9:9.
8. Matthew 9:37–38.
9. Matthew chapter 10.
10. Matthew 10:5–33
11. King, "Out of the Long Night," 14.

In his last words in Matthew's Gospel Jesus announces, "All authority in heaven and on earth has been given to me."[12] What does "all authority" mean? Jesus is of the lineage of Abraham and King David, he is Messiah, God with us, an amazing rabbi/teacher, one who stands among the prophets, but is greater than them. He is the new Moses, leading God's people to the promised land of the kingdom. He has the authority to forgive and heal, and the authority to correct as he drives out the extortionate businessmen from the temple. He is the crucified, resurrected Lord, hurt and healed. He has the authority of one who has suffered injustice, who has descended into hell to redeem the captives there.[13] There is no one and nowhere that cannot be reached, touched, and loved by Jesus.

Jesus embodies the Sermon on the Mount in word, deed, and Spirit. The Sermon on the Mount is not just 111 verses of sublime Scripture. It is Jesus. His recalled words, read with illuminating Spirit, can challenge, enlighten, and disciple us. As we learn and embody the Sermon on the Mount, then we can begin to teach with authority people of every race and tribe, extending Jesus' kingdom, and transforming this world.

REFLECTION

1. What kind of authority do you see Jesus showing? How does the kind of authority that Jesus demonstrates change how we normally understand authority?

2. What do you think of the idea that Jesus is the embodiment of the Sermon on the Mount? How do you see Jesus living out this teaching?

3. What does it mean for us to be sent out like sheep amidst wolves with the message of the kingdom? What does it say about the reality of our world, and the nature of the kingdom?

4. Are we, like the first apostles, commissioned as Sermon on the Mount disciples to make, baptize, and teach new disciples from every ethnic group, every tribe, every nation throughout the world (Matthew 28:19–20)? How do you feel about this task? How can we personally prepare? How do we support each other doing this? What will be the fruit of this great and marvelous work?

---

12. Matthew 28:18.
13. See the Apostles' Creed and also Ephesians 4:9 and 1 Peter 3:18–20.

After Words

5. Having read and meditated on the 111 verses of the Sermon on the Mount, what are you thinking now? Are your thoughts positive or negative or a mixture of both? Are you feeling called to move towards a deeper kind of discipleship? Is that both a joy and a struggle? What might be your first step? Who can you walk with?

Write your thoughts down, whatever they might be . . .

Prayer Thought

Help us sense your authority Lord Jesus, greater than any earthly authority, commissioning us to take your message of peace, justice, grace, and gentleness into all the world. Help us be the living, practicing example of all your teachings. In your name, Amen.

PART THREE

Living the Sermon on the Mount in Difficult Times

22

Early Christian Times and Living the Sermon on the Mount

"The Romans are the plunderers of the world . . . If the enemy is rich, they are rapacious, if poor they lust for dominion. Not East, not West has sated them. . . . They rob, butcher, plunder, and call it 'empire'; and where they make a desolation, they call it 'peace.'"

— SCOTTISH CHIEFTAIN (IN TACITUS)[1]

Early Christians knew firsthand the terrible violence of the Roman Empire. At least three of the four Gospels were written after the unsuccessful Jewish Revolt of 66–70 CE. The kingdom that Jesus proclaimed was very different from the empire of Caesar. No early church leader endorsed Christians participating in warfare for the first three centuries.[2] Early Christians had no illusions about Rome and its oppressive cruelty, nor about violent revolt as a remedy.[3]

So, in this historical context of violence, Jesus' teachings of love your enemy are remarkable. Non-retaliation is taught over thirty times in the whole New Testament, so this teaching is not only found in the Sermon

---

1. Cited in Horsley, *Jesus and Empire*, 15.
2. Driver, *How Christians Made Peace*, 14.
3. Driver, *How Christians Made Peace*, 14–15.

Part Three | Living the Sermon on the Mount in Difficult Times

on the Mount.[4] Themes of the Sermon on the Mount are repeated in the Sermon on the Plain in Luke, and also found in the Letter of James and in Paul's First Letter to the Corinthians, Romans, as well as other first-century writings like the Didache and First and Second Clement.[5]

The importance of the Sermon on the Mount in the early church can also be seen in how often it is quoted by early Christian writers. Warren S. Kissinger provides a good summary:

> No portion of the Scriptures was more frequently quoted and referred to by the Ante-Nicene writers than the Sermon on the Mount. The fifth chapter of Matthew appears more often in their works than any other single chapter, and Matthew 5–7 more frequently than any other three chapters in the entire Bible.[6]

Origen (c. 184–c. 253), one of the most influential early Christian theologians and a prolific writer, saw the Sermon quite straightforwardly as something to be obeyed. Jesus, argued Origen, "conveys no other meaning than this, that it is in our power to observe what is commanded. And there we are rightly rendered liable to condemnation if we transgress those commandments which we are able to keep."[7] Cyprian, in his work *Ad Quirinium*, cites the Sermon on the Mount twenty-eight times.[8]

Thus, for the early Christians the Sermon on the Mount was a central and important teaching. It was important in a very thorough discipleship formation process that perhaps lasted at least three years before baptism.[9] Alan Kreider talks about a process of learning that formed new habits based on new values in those seeking to become Christians. It was by the way they lived that Christians attracted others:

> It was not Christian worship that attracted outsiders; it was Christians who attracted them, and outsiders found the Christians attractive because of the Christian habitus, which catechesis and worship had formed.[10]

---

4. Gordon Zerbe, cited in Swartley, *Covenant of Peace*, 409.
5. Grant, "Sermon on the Mount," 215–16.
6. Kissinger, *Sermon on the Mount*, 6.
7. Heim, "Sermon on the Mount," 66.
8. Kreider, *Patient Ferment*, 161.
9. Kreider, *Patient Ferment*, 177.
10. Kreider, *Patient Ferment*, 135.

Early Christian Times and Living the Sermon on the Mount

Early Christians were not superficially Christian. They had to endure at least ten periods of major persecution beginning with the Emperor Nero 64–68 and ending with the greatest persecution of all by the Emperor Diocletian 303–311. It was in the first persecution by Nero that traditionally the apostles Peter and Paul are thought to have been martyred.[11] Despite persecution, some scholars estimate that by 300 CE, Christians had grown to between 8–12 percent of the Roman Empire.[12]

Ronald J. Sider compiled all the relevant early Christian texts up to the Council of Nicaea in 325. From compiling, reading, and analyzing all the relevant ancient manuscripts, here are Sider's conclusions:

> Nine different Christian writers in sixteen different treatises say that killing is wrong. No extant Christian writing before Constantine argues that there is any circumstance under which a Christian may kill ... Matthew 5:38–48 is probably the most frequently cited biblical text in the writings collected here. At least ten different writers in at least twenty-eight different places cite or refer to this biblical passage and note that Christians love their enemies and turn the other cheek.[13]

Thus, the early Christians opposed killing as a soldier, capital punishment, infanticide, exposure of babies, abortion, and gladiatorial contests. Christians were taught not to watch gladiatorial contests—killing as entertainment was not an option. Alan Kreider eloquently makes a case that early Christians taught, learned, and practiced patience. This is a virtue wedded to nonviolence and includes love of enemies.[14]

There is evidence that Christians did begin to serve in the army in small numbers from 173 CE and the number slowly increased, so not all Christians were obedient to these teachings, although some soldiers had more police than war functions. As Christians, they were still not allowed to kill even if serving in the army.[15] There are at least four soldiers who

---

11. Rigoli and Cummings, "Vatican Chronicles," line 26.

12. Kreider, *Patient Ferment*, 8. However, not all scholars agree on this level of growth.

13. Sider, ed., *Early Church on Killing*, 168, 171.

14. Alan Kreider's last book has patience as its grand theme and title: *The Patient Ferment of the Early Church*.

15. For instance Sider, ed., *Early Church on Killing*, 185.

were martyred for refusing to work in the military before Constantine became emperor.[16]

REFLECTIONS

1. How would you describe the early church in a few words?
2. What impresses you about discipleship in the early church?
3. What are consistencies about discipleship in the teachings of the Sermon on the Mount, the rest of the New Testament, and the early church for the first 300 years? Are there inconsistencies?
4. How would life in the early church be the same, but also different, to your own church experience?
5. What can we learn from the early church about following Jesus in discipleship?

Prayer Thought

Loving God, thank you for the faith of the first Christians. Help us learn from them. Amen.

---

16. Sider, *Early Church on Killing*, 152–58. Marinus was martyred in 260, Maximilian in 295, Marcellus in 298, and Julius in 304.

23

Christendom Times

Fusion of Christianity with Empire

THE EMPEROR CONSTANTINE

The story of Christendom begins on the site of York Minster, not far from where I grew up. Today York Minster is a very impressive church building, one of the largest of its kind in North Europe, a classic monument to Christendom. It is the seat of the Archbishop of York, the third highest office of the Church of England, after the monarch as Supreme Governor and the Archbishop of Canterbury. It was on this site, then pagan, in 306 that Constantine on the death of his father was proclaimed emperor of part of the Roman Empire. Next to today's York Minster, there is an impressive bronze statue of Constantine celebrating this momentous event. On one side are the words:

CONSTANTINE THE GREAT
AD 274–337
PROCLAIMED ROMAN EMPEROR
IN YORK AD 306

The statue of Constantine, in full battle dress, has him looking thoughtfully at his sword, the tip of which is broken. At the front of the statue, below the broken sword, are these words:

CONSTANTINE BY THIS SIGN CONQUER

Part Three | Living the Sermon on the Mount in Difficult Times

What happened next? After a series of military conquests, Constantine arrived in Rome in 312 to attack rival Emperor Maxentius. If Constantine were to win, he would become the sole emperor of the West. The stakes were high. Christian historian Eusebius of Caesarea, a fan and contemporary of Constantine, tells the story that on the eve of the battle, Constantine had a vision of the cross in the sky with Greek words saying "In this [sign], conquer." Encouraged, according to Eusebius's account, Constantine conquered. By 324 Constantine ruled the whole Roman Empire, east and west, until his death in 337.

For Constantine had the cross become a sword?

Emperor Constantine granted official toleration of Christians in the Edict of Milan in 313 CE. This was a huge relief, for Christians were just emerging from the Diocletian persecution that began in 303 and was the worst of all persecutions in the early church. Constantine was open to Christianity, and although unbaptized, he engaged as the equivalent of a bishop in the Council of Nicaea discussions on the nature of Christ and his relationship with God the Father, in 325 CE. The Nicaean Creed is part of Orthodox, Anglican, and Catholic worship still today.

Constantine is celebrated as the first Christian emperor. What was he really like? Was his discipleship godly, faithful to the Jesus of the Gospels? Did he love his enemies as the Sermon on the Mount commands? The statue of Constantine by York Minster has the tip of his sword broken, suggesting he became less violent. Did this really happen?

Constantine, in fact, remained as ruthless, impatient, and violent as any previous Roman emperor. A year after participating in the Council of Nicaea he had his father-in-law, son Crispus, and his wife Fausta executed. In his reign he increased the use of torture and capital punishment.[1] Constantine was finally baptized just before he died in 337, but he had not subjected himself to the same rigorous discipleship formation process that was usual in the early church.[2] Was he ever really converted?

DEFINING CHRISTENDOM

"[T]he church-empire merger."[3]

---

1. Kreider, *Patient Ferment*, 264; Murray, *Post-Christendom*, 30.
2. See Kreider, *Patient Ferment*, chapter 9.
3. Nugent, "Yoderian Rejoinder," 1.

> "[T]he fusion of church and state most evident in the church's willingness to use the empire or state's coercive power structures—particularly the sword—to assist in the church's mission."[4]

Christendom was birthed as an imperial church under Roman Emperors Constantine (reigned 306–337) and Theodosius I (reigned 379–395).[5] The North African theologian Augustine (354–430) was the founding theological architect of Christendom.

What did Christendom mean? It meant expanding and controlling lands, populations, and cultures. In Christendom, Christianity changed from a minority to a majority church. It also became a partner of empire.[6]

Christendom meant the use of violence by government on behalf of Catholic Nicene orthodoxy. Later this was also continued in both Eastern Orthodoxy and Roman Catholicism after the 1054 schism, and then after the Protestant Reformation beginning in 1517, with national Protestant churches like Lutheranism, the Church of England, and Calvinism.

Christendom in Europe is a legal structure, whether Catholic or Protestant in expression. For example, the British monarch is legally the supreme governor of the Church of England. In Canada, and especially the US, Christendom is expressed more subtly in a context where there is official separation of church and state. Christendom is expressed culturally, in ideas, and socially. Christianity and Americanism in the nineteenth century merged into a single kind of spirituality.[7]

CHRISTENDOM MEANT VIOLENCE

Christendom was founded on the marriage between the state and church giving the church privileges in return for the church's ideological support of the state. Sometimes it is helpful to talk about this process of change, from early Christianity to Christendom Christianity, as the Constantinian shift.[8] Sometimes it is called the Christendom shift.[9]

---

4. Nugent, "Yoderian Rejoinder", 5.
5. Hall, *End of Christendom*, 1.
6. Hall, *End of Christendom*, 13, 19.
7. Hall, *End of Christendom*, 29, 30.
8. John H. Yoder, for instance, talks about the Constantinian shift. See Yoder, *Christian Attitudes to War*, 37–54.
9. For example, see Murray, *Post-Christendom*, chapter 4.

Part Three | Living the Sermon on the Mount in Difficult Times

Discipleship became superficial. Baby baptism became common as the church changed to be the official and imposed religion for everyone. The Sermon on the Mount still applied to clergy and monastics, but not to lay people. Clergy and monastics could not kill or go to war, but lay people could.[10]

Increasingly, pagans, dissident Christians, and also Jews were persecuted. St. Augustine misused the words of Jesus, "compel people to come in,"[11] to justify coercion and persecution to enforce conformity with developing institutional Catholicism.[12] Augustine vigorously lobbied Rome and the imperial court in Ravenna to crush a teaching called Pelagianism. This included sending a bribe of eighty African stallions to courtiers.[13] Augustine is the prime mover of coercion to enforce the unity of the church. In later centuries, it resulted in great tragedy for pagans, dissenting Christians, and for Jews.[14] Augustine laid the egg of coercion that hatched crusades and inquisition. Some argue that here, expanded by Protestant Reformer Martin Luther, are the origins of the Nazi Holocaust of the Jews.[15] The culture of Christendom was authoritarian and totalitarian, and did not allow for dissent or pluralism.[16] Augustine saw the possibility of the conversion of the whole world, but it was to be aided by violence.

With the teachings of St. Augustine, Christians were given permission to use violence in war through the emerging just war tradition.[17] Christian judges could execute, and also torture, in an investigation to establish the truth.[18]

---

10. For Ambrose on these subjects, see Bainton, *Christian Attitudes toward War and Peace*, 91. For Aquinas, see Gill, *Textbook of Christian Ethics*, 285.

11. Luke 14:23

12. Murray, *Post-Christendom*, chapters 2–5. Murray provides an excellent review in these chapters.

13. Kreider, *Patient Ferment*, 281.

14. Murray, *Post-Christendom*, 64–5.

15. Landau, *Nazi Holocaust*, 46–47.

16. Murray, *Post-Christendom*, 56.

17. See Bainton, *Christian Attitudes toward War and Peace*, 33–43, 89–93. For Aquinas's summary of Augustine's three criteria for a just war see Aquinas, "War, Christians and the Clergy" in Gill, *Textbook of Christian Ethics*, 281–82.

18. Augustine argued that the judge is not guilty of sin using torture with these words, "If it is through unavoidable ignorance and the unavoidable duty of judging that he tortures the innocent, then he himself is certainly not guilty." See Augustine, *City of God*, Book XIX, chapter 6, 928.

James Carroll, a former Roman Catholic priest, sums up the impact of Constantine and Augustine for the church:

> When the power of the Empire became joined to the ideology of the Church, the Empire was immediately recast and reenergized, and the Church became an entity so different from what had preceded it was to be almost unrecognizable. It goes without saying that the conversion of Constantine, for Church and Empire, both, led to consequences better and worse—although not for Jews, for whom, from this, nothing good would come.[19]

If Constantine laid the political foundations of Christendom, St. Augustine was its conceptual architect, its first brilliant and enduring chief theologian.[20] Unlike the early church, where patience was a primary virtue of the Christian life, Augustine justified impatience, like a Roman ruler.[21] Augustine shaped decisively Western Christianity, both Catholicism and later Protestantism, for perhaps blessing, but also for great tragedy.

Discipleship changed from kingdom of God citizenship, with Christ as Lord and King, to being loyal, obedient, and patriotic subjects of local lords and monarchs. Heaven after this life became the focus, rather than heaven on earth in the coming kingdom of God. Salvation was pie in the sky later, rather than daily bread for all now on earth.[22]

The Holy Wars of the Crusades, launched by Pope Urban II in 1095, were against Islam and to gain control of Jerusalem and the Holy Land. In Jerusalem, blood ran knee deep when the crusaders attacked. Jews and heretics were also slaughtered during this period. The crusades continued to 1291, a year after Jews were expelled from England. Church historian Roland Bainton argued:

> The crusading idea requires that the cause shall be holy (and no cause is more holy than religion), that the war shall be fought under God and with his help, that the crusaders shall be godly and their enemies ungodly, and the war shall be prosecuted unsparingly.[23]

---

19. Carroll, *Constantine's Sword*, 171.
20. Murray, *Post-Christendom*, 60.
21. Kreider, *Patient Ferment*, chapter 10.
22. Murray, *Post-Christendom*, 68, and riffing off the Lord's Prayer.
23. Bainton, *Christian Attitudes toward War and Peace*, 148.

Part Three | Living the Sermon on the Mount in Difficult Times

American Catholic ethicist Lisa Sowle Cahill adds, "The crusades . . . place violence (and especially killing) at the heart, not the periphery of faithful discipleship."[24]

Monastics kept alive the practice of living out the Sermon on the Mount. St. Francis (c. 1181–1226) is also an inspiring figure. Franciscans today have a reputation for concern about poverty, a commitment to ecology, and to interfaith dialogue. St. Francis was also a former soldier, and part of his conversion was a commitment to nonviolence. The Beatitudes are very important for Franciscans.

REFLECTIONS

1. What was the Emperor Constantine like? If you were a Christian in 315 CE, what might you be saying about him? Looking back now, how did he change Christianity?

2. In your own words say what is meant by Christendom. What was good or bad about it?

3. What was the theological contribution of Augustine to Christendom?

4. What might Jews, Muslims, or a "heretical" Christian say about Christendom?

5. Compare the place of the Sermon on the Mount in the early church with its place in Christendom after Constantine and Augustine. What are your conclusions?

Prayer Thought

Loving Father, was Christendom something you approved of, or was it a betrayal of the work of your Son? Help us learn from this period of church history and thus be better disciples of your Son Jesus. Amen.

---

24. Cahill, *Love Your Enemies*, 122, 123, 125.

24

Protestant Times
Christendom Continued

We cannot understand the Protestant Reformation without understanding Augustine. Augustine, as we have noted, is a theological giant in Western Christianity, a saint for Catholics, Anglicans, and (outside the West) the Eastern Orthodox Church. Protestant Reformers Martin Luther and John Calvin drew on his work in terms of salvation and grace. Augustine also took seriously the Sermon on the Mount.[1] He wrote the first commentary on the Sermon on the Mount in Christian history,[2] and said it was "the perfect measure of the Christian life."[3] However, as already indicated, Augustine was not good about loving his enemies. Were Protestant Reformers Luther, Calvin, and Henry VIII any better?

MARTIN LUTHER

Martin Luther (1483–1546) was the courageous first Protestant who began the Reformation. He was a German Augustinian monk, and so was familiar with Augustine's thought, drawing particularly on his theology of grace.

Luther preached on the Sermon on the Mount in 1530–32, and these sermons were written down by his students and later published. He argued that living the Sermon on the Mount did not mean you could earn your

---

1. Wilken, "Augustine," 43–57.
2. Augustine, *Our Lord's Sermon on the Mount*.
3. Guelich, "Interpreting the Sermon on the Mount."

salvation. Rather, living the Sermon on the Mount was a fruit of justification, the fruit of the unmerited gift of grace through faith in Christ.

Sometimes it is suggested that for Luther, the Sermon on the Mount was an impossible standard; it was law meant to drive us in despair to God's grace.[4] Against this position of an impossible standard, there are no words in the Sermon on the Mount that suggest this teaching is impossible. The Sermon on the Mount speaks of *doing* more twenty times.[5] Luther is trying to trump Matthew with Paul.[6] There is a tension between the Paul of Galatians, and Jesus of Matthew's Gospel, as Hans Dieter Betz has pointed out.[7] However, both Galatians and the Sermon on the Mount talk about the importance of fruit in the life of a disciple, and both indicate God's grace. Before and after the Sermon on the Mount are Jesus' gracious actions, including healing with no requirement but need. Thus, the Sermon on the Mount is set in the middle of a story of God's love, where grace abounds. One has to read the Sermon on the Mount in the context of the whole of Matthew's Gospel, and throughout the Gospel God's grace is abundant.[8]

Key to understanding Luther's teaching on the Sermon on the Mount is his two-kingdom theology. The person of faith lived in two worlds, both under God. First was a Christian world that was personal and included church life, where the Sermon on the Mount could be lived. Second, there was a secular world ruled by monarch or prince, where the sword should be used to restrain evil. Thus, a Christian might be a shopkeeper, peasant farmer, judge, soldier, ruler, or even executioner. While the Christian's inner attitude was informed by the Sermon on the Mount, the actions of the Christian in official secular capacities could be different. In the secular world, evil was restrained by the force of the state, and a Christian might

---

4. Schrock, "3 Ways to Misread the Sermon on the Mount." See also Davies and Allison, "Reflections on the Sermon on the Mount," 290.

5. Davies and Allison, "Reflections on the Sermon on the Mount," 291.

6. Davies and Allison, "Reflections on the Sermon on the Mount," 290.

7. Betz and Schweiker, "Concerning Mountains and Morals," 12.

8. Galatians 5:22–23; Matthew 7:15–20. Notice that love, peace, kindness, gentleness, and self-control are among the fruit of the Spirit in Galatians. In Matthew, the kingdom of heaven proclaimed by Jesus comes as a gift or grace, and the first four Beatitudes are promises of grace for the poor, those who mourn, the meek, and those who hunger and thirst (Matthew 4:17, 5:3–6). We are to love our enemies because the Father gracefully loves good and bad alike (Matthew 5:45). So, though, the word *grace* is not used in the Sermon on the Mount, it is abundantly implied. We are to live the Sermon on the Mount in response to God's grace. See again Davies and Allison Jr., "Reflections on the Sermon on the Mount," 299.

fully engage in this in order to love and protect their neighbor. Thus, the believer fulfilling their societal role might go to court, sentence someone to death as a judge, lead a people to war as a ruler, or kill as a soldier. However, a soldier could not fight in an unjust war.[9] In Luther's thought, the Christian has a dual citizenship: "subject to Christ through faith, and to the emperor through his body."[10] In Luther's thought are echoes of the tension in Augustine's theology of inconsistency between inner disposition and outer action in the context of the fusion of church and government in Christendom.[11]

What fruits do we see of Luther? Both Augustine and Luther are strong on the centrality of grace for salvation. However, both lack grace to others—they do not love their enemies very much. Their theologies are ideologies in the service of the powerful whom they serve. Luther's two-kingdom theology meant historically that Lutheranism has been conservative socially, politically, theologically, and in terms of wealth.[12] His theology lacked a prophetic social justice challenge to society. Luther was brutal about putting down the 1524-25 German Peasants' Revolt. He said, "Therefore, let everyone who can, smite, slay, and stab, secretly or openly, remembering that nothing can be more poisonous, hurtful, or devilish than a rebel."[13] Luther's extended rants of hate of Jews,[14] according to Jewish scholars, prepared the way 400 years later for the Nazi holocaust.[15] In recent decades, the deep repentance of Lutherans from this tragic heritage is to be noted and appreciated.[16]

JOHN CALVIN

John Calvin (1509-1564) was a brilliant intellectual, and through his written work, especially the *Institutes*, a very influential Protestant teacher. Calvin lived most of his ministerial life in Geneva, Switzerland. With Ulrich Zwingli he represents the initial Reform Protestant tradition growing out of Swiss city-states. Like Luther, Calvin was influenced by Augustine,

9. Stephenson, "Two Governments," end of section 9.
10. Cited in Stephenson, "Two Governments," note 28.
11. See Stephenson, "Two Governments," 326-28, 332.
12. Nauert, "Tore Meistad," 572.
13. Luther, "Against the Robbing and Murdering Hordes of Peasants," 50.
14. Luther, "On the Jews and Their Lies."
15. Landau, *Nazi Holocaust*, 46-47.
16. Marans, "On Luther and His Lies."

especially on the teaching of grace. There is some discussion as to whether Geneva was a theocracy during Calvin's time of living and teaching there; Calvin certainly had a great deal of influence. He spoke against Catholics, Jews, and Anabaptists, as did Luther.

For Calvin as for Luther, there was to be no difference between clergy and ordinary Christians, so the Sermon on the Mount was for all. Insightfully, Calvin sees the Sermon on the Mount as a collection of sayings rather than a real sermon. In his commentary he is typically thorough, giving a detailed exposition for every few verses in twenty-seven units.[17] He sought to be moderate, steering a middle way between what he saw as false extremes, yet he also softened some of the demands of Jesus' teaching. Some oath-taking was acceptable. On turning the other cheek, he suggested it was foolish to continue to be hit. Of course, you should go to court to defend what is yours, otherwise you encourage dishonest men.[18]

Did Calvin love his enemies? He advocated for the execution of Michael Servetus for his heretical teachings on the Trinity. In 1555 he supported the execution of a number of plotters involved in an attempted insurrection in Geneva.

THE BIRTH OF THE CHURCH OF ENGLAND— A POLITICAL REVOLUTION

The Protestant Reformation in England was different from Protestant Reformations elsewhere in Europe. It was not a religious but a political revolution first and foremost, and initiated not by monk or preacher, but by a king.[19] King Henry VIII replaced the pope's authority in England by making himself the supreme governor of the Church of England in 1534.[20] The king was aided by the politically skillful Thomas Cromwell, until his downfall from Henry VIII's favor in 1540.[21]

To evaluate the first years of the English Reformation, it is important to understand the character of Henry VIII in his long reign from 1509 to 1547. As head of the church was he a faithful servant of God, a disciple of Jesus?

17. Spencer, "John Calvin," 133–34.
18. Spencer, "John Calvin," 143, 137, 140–41.
19. Chadwick, *Reformation*, 97.
20. Chadwick, *Reformation*, 101.
21. Chadwick, *Reformation*, 100–116.

He was married six times in a desperate quest for a male heir. He executed two of his wives—Anne Boleyn and Catherine Howard—and thus was guilty of domestic violence. He executed people like Thomas More and John Fisher, who did not agree with Henry's divorce, or making himself supreme governor of the Church of England. In his reign, between 57,000 and 72,000 people were executed.[22] He dissolved the monasteries and confiscated their lands to add to his own wealth and to reward favorites. Monasteries were a safety net for the poor, so when Henry VIII privatized ten million acres of good farmland, he forever broke the monastic safety net for the poor and further impoverished them. This also led to a further concentration of land ownership that troubles British society to this day.[23]

It would appear that Henry VIII, as founder of a nationalized English Christendom, was as violent, cruel, and unfaithful as the Roman Emperor Constantine ten centuries earlier. The Church of England has dominated the English religious, cultural, and geographical landscape with steepled churches and cathedrals all over the land. The monarch continues as supreme governor down to today, and the state church is privileged with power and advantage in many ways.

All Anglican clergy must commit to the Thirty-Nine Articles.[24] There is no article endorsing or even mentioning the Sermon on the Mount. Article thirty-five lists homilies (sermons) on twenty-one topics, but the Sermon on the Mount again is not mentioned. The last three articles are of particular interest because they arguably contradict the spirit and teaching of Jesus in the Sermon on the Mount. They support war, the death penalty, private property, and oath-taking. Thus, the Anglican church was well-positioned to bless monarchy, the rich, emerging capitalism, the enclosure movement (converting centuries-old common land to new private ownership), and the beginning British Empire.

REFLECTIONS

1. What are your reactions to the stories of Luther, Calvin, and Henry VIII?

---

22. Layton, "Top 10 Heads That Rolled."
23. Standing, *Plunder of the Commons*, 11.
24. Church of England, "Articles of Religion."

Part Three | Living the Sermon on the Mount in Difficult Times

2. In the North of England, harvests had been bad in 1534 and food prices nearly doubled. What would your thoughts have been if you were poor in the North of England at the time of the dissolution of the monasteries, and you no longer had this safety net? Would you have protested against Henry VIII's actions or stayed home?

3. Lutheranism became the state church in parts of Germany and in the Scandinavian countries. Calvinism became the state church in Scotland and the Netherlands. The Church of England became the state church in England. Christendom in North Europe became Protestant and was nationalized. Christendom was no longer Catholic in all of Europe. Was this a good or a bad thing? What was lost, and what was gained?

4. What is your response to the Anglican Thirty-Nine Articles and their relationship to the Sermon on the Mount?

Prayer Thought

Loving God, your Son wept over Jerusalem because the people did not understand what made for peace. He must have wept over Christendom, Protestant and Catholic too. Help us in our difficult times to learn what makes for peace. Amen.

25

Protestant Times

Dissenter Protest and Nonconformity

There were dissenters against state churches, and in Britain they were later called Nonconformists. In England and Wales they included Congregationalists, Baptists, Quakers, and Methodists. In their congregational life, they were strongly democratic, modeled the British culture of loyal opposition, and also strongly influenced Christian and political expressions in the United States.

Nonconformists suffered for their stands of conscience, initially by imprisonment or worse. It was not until the nineteenth century in Britain that they could stand for public office, work for the civil service, or be awarded degrees from Oxford and Cambridge. The dissenter story begins with the Anabaptists in Switzerland. How did Anabaptists and other dissenters challenge Catholic and Protestant Christendoms?

THE ANABAPTISTS

The Anabaptists are sometimes called the radical, or left wing, of the Protestant Reformation, and began in 1525, just after the German Peasants' Revolt in 1524–25. The Anabaptist family includes the Swiss Brethren historically, the communal Hutterites, Mennonites, the Amish, and Brethren. They failed to get established in Britain, but today there is an Anabaptist Network.

Part Three | Living the Sermon on the Mount in Difficult Times

The central practice of the Anabaptists was reading the Bible together. They were Christ-centered. They listened to and followed Jesus:

> The Sermon on the Mount was not a wonderful collection of unattainable ideals but a guide for daily living. They reconnected spirituality and discipleship: in the words of Han Denck, "No one can know Christ unless he follows after him in life . . ." However, the dissidents' conviction that following Jesus meant applying his teaching in ways that challenged political, economic, and social norms provoked persecution.[1]

One beginning of Anabaptism was in Zurich, Switzerland in 1525, when Conrad Grebel baptized George Blaurock, who then baptized others. Although they had been baptized as infants, they were now rebaptized as an expression of faith. *Anabaptist* means rebaptizers, and it was a revolutionary step. They followed what they believed to be the true pattern in the New Testament—voluntary believer's baptism. Catholics and the new Protestant Reformers, including Martin Luther, Ulrich Zwingli, and later John Calvin, disagreed with them profoundly. Throughout Europe, rebaptism meant the death penalty—a law that went back to the Justinian Code, 529 CE.[2] As a result, Anabaptists were persecuted by both Catholics and Protestants. Over 3,000 Anabaptists were executed, and many more sent to prison or made refugees.[3]

From the beginning, the Anabaptists took the Sermon on the Mount seriously. It should be practiced without compromise in this life, believing God's grace made it possible.[4] If Catholics were about "works," and Reformers were about "faith," then Anabaptists expressed both faith and works, that is faith to follow Jesus as teacher, example, and Savior in discipleship. Michael Sattler, an early Anabaptist leader and former Benedictine prior, called the Anabaptist way a "middle path".[5]

Discipleship meant living out the Sermon on the Mount faithfully, taking it literally. In 1524, Conrad Grebel exemplified the love of enemies with these words in a letter to Thomas Müntzer, a leader of the German Peasants' Revolt:

---

1. Murray, *Post-Christendom*, 121.
2. Friedman, "Anabaptism."
3. Murray, *Post-Christendom*, 117.
4. Bender, "Anabaptist Vision."
5. Murray, *Post-Christendom*, 121–22.

> True Christians use neither worldly sword nor engage in war, since among them taking human life has ceased entirely, for we are no longer under the Old Covenant... The Gospel and those who accept it are not to be protected with the sword, neither should they thus protect themselves.[6]

The first Anabaptist statement of faith was the Schleitheim Confession of 1527, drafted by Michael Sattler. It describes practical discipleship and how to organize a congregation. Its seven articles include two teachings from the Sermon on the Mount. The sword is outside the perfection of Christ, and only the ban, not violence, may be used to discipline a wayward church member. Oath-making is against the teaching of Christ.[7]

As to what parts of the Sermon on the Mount are quoted by Anabaptist writers, Abe Duerk summarizes as follows:

> The Beatitudes are cited quite frequently, especially Matthew 5:10–12 (in relation to the Anabaptists' experience of suffering and persecution). Other references which are cited most frequently are Matthew 5:33–37 (integrity and the oath); Matthew 5:38–48 (nonresistance and love of enemies); Matthew 6:24 (serving God or mammon); Matthew 6:33 (seeking first the kingdom of God); Matthew 7:1–14 (the narrow way); Matthew 7:15–20 (false prophets are known by their fruits); and Matthew 7:21–23 (doing the will of the Father).[8]

Loving enemies and not making oaths are Anabaptist distinctives that are quoted most often. The Anabaptists were pioneers in religious liberty. They were the first reformers to insist on separation of church and state and thus seek the end of Christendom, and a return to the model of early Christianity.

GEORGE FOX AND THE SOCIETY OF FRIENDS (QUAKERS)

George Fox was born in 1624 in the village now called Fenny Drayton, fifteen miles southwest of Leicester, England. A seeker for truth and God, Fox did not find much help from Church of England priests, or ministers

---

6. Cited in Bender, "Anabaptist Vision," note 55.
7. Schleitheim Confession, Articles VI and VII.
8. Dueck," Sermon on the Mount."

from dissenting churches like the Baptists. Suffering recurring spiritual depression, he finally had a breakthrough that he described in these words:

> And when all my hopes in them and in all men were gone, so that I had nothing outwardly to help me, nor could tell what to do, then, oh, then, I heard a voice which said, "There is one, even Christ Jesus, that can speak to thy condition"; and when I heard it my heart did leap for joy.[9]

Fox was thus moved to follow the Spirit of Christ, and taught this to others. His early spiritual seeking was at the time of the English Civil War (1642–1652), a conflict between Charles I and Parliament. The Quaker movement began to significantly expand after the end of the English Civil War in 1652. It is perhaps easier to see the importance of the nonviolence of Jesus when the failure and destructiveness of violence is so clearly understood by many people from their firsthand experience.

The Quakers have had an enormous influence for justice and peace in the world during the more than 350 years of their existence. For example, Quakers have been in the forefront of prison reform. With others like William Wilberforce, they played a major role in the abolition of the slave trade and ending slavery itself. They have stood against war, been leading conscientious objectors, and helped play a part in peace agreements including in Northern Ireland. Quaker businesses like Rowntree's, Fry, and Cadbury's were model employers and leaders in philanthropic work. Quakers have been involved in the founding of many organizations doing good in our world, including Oxfam, Greenpeace, and Amnesty International.[10] In 1947, Quakers were awarded the Nobel Peace Prize for their work to relieve suffering and feed many millions of starving people during and after both world wars.[11] The largest academic peace studies department in the world is at Bradford University, and the professorial chair was originally funded by Quakers.

Fox frequently used the phrase "that of God in everyone" in his pastoral ministry, as evidenced in his journal and letters.[12] One of the most famous versions of this phrase is "Walk cheerfully over the world, answering that of God in everyone."[13] Walk cheerfully over the world means to work

---

9. Ingle, *First Among Friends*, 49. Fox, *Journal*, 11.
10. Rickerman, "Twentieth Century."
11. "Quakers and the Nobel Peace Prize."
12. Benson, "'That of God in Every Man.'"
13. Fox, "Letter to Quaker Ministers."

cheerfully against the injustice of human systems that betray human dignity. This emphasis on the equal worth of all persons has led many Quakers to advocate for human equality.

The Quakers have sought to listen to the Spirit of Christ from the beginning. Some have been informed by the Sermon on the Mount in Matthew's Gospel, or found confirmation in it. The Quakers, along with Anabaptists, and Church of the Brethren, belong to what is called the historic peace churches.

JOHN WESLEY

John Wesley (1703–1791), with his brother Charles, was the founder of Methodism. John preached and Charles wrote wonderful hymns. John Wesley was an innovative organizer of discipling through the class meeting, and a persuasive outdoor preacher, with the world as his parish. Wesley died an Anglican, but he created a Nonconformist church.

Wesley preached often on the Sermon on the Mount. His second written sermon was "Seek first the kingdom of God . . ." (Matthew 6:33) from the Sermon on the Mount. He preached this sermon ten to twelve times between 1725 and 1727. When he returned from two years in America, he preached on the Sermon on the Mount over 100 times between 1739 and 1746. Thus, the Sermon on the Mount was first taught outdoors by Jesus, and Wesley preached it a great deal outdoors also.[14]

Like Luther and Paul, Wesley preached justification by faith, and like Paul he also taught sanctification—growing in holiness.[15] As Mark Noll aptly puts it, for Wesley, "Christ came into the world to save sinners, but also to equip them for holy living."[16] Sanctification is progressive change of character, overcoming sin in a believer's life, through grace and the Holy Spirit. Wesley was critical of Luther's two-kingdom teaching, and rejected the idea that a Christian was simultaneously a saint and sinner. And Wesley's teaching of sanctification was not just personal, but had social implications as well—like abolishing slavery.[17] The upside-down kingdom of God meant challenging the injustices of society. Social as well as personal salvation was

---

14. Noll, "John Wesley," 153–55.

15. For Paul's teaching on sanctification see for example 1 Thessalonians 5:23; Galatians 5:22–23, and Romans 6:1–2, 15–23.

16. Noll, "John Wesley," 163–64.

17. Nauert, "Tore Meistad," 572.

possible. To quote Noll, "'Gospel obedience' was the key phrase, since it communicated deep commitment to both salvation by grace through faith, and holiness in obedience to God's will."[18]

Two hundred years later, Morgan Phillips, when secretary of the Labour Party, said British socialism owed more to Methodism than it did to Marxism. We should actually credit all British nonconformity.[19] British socialism was Christian and rooted in faith not atheism. It was inspired by Moses and Jesus rather than Marx and Engels. It drew on the Bible rather than *Das Kapital*, with a vision of the kingdom of God on earth rather than a communist utopia. Its revolution was led by the democratically elected Clement Atlee and the Labour party in 1945, rather than the violent overthrow of the Russian Czar by Lenin and the Bolsheviks in 1917. The result was the welfare state, including free medical treatment for all, and that still continues. After all, Jesus did not charge for healing.

Using the Sermon on the Mount, Wesley was sharply critical of "Christian kingdoms that are tearing out each other's bowels, desolating one another with fire and sword," and doing this in the name of the Prince of Peace as they waged war in front of Jews, Turks, and pagans.[20] He argued also for simplicity of life, of being content with enough, and generously sharing with others. In Wesley's thought, there is a real tension between capitalism and faithful discipleship. Wesley was a disciple who lived the Sermon on the Mount and helped thousands of others live it as well. For Wesley, God's grace is unlimited, and the gospel offers great hope in a world of sin. Living the Sermon on the Mount can be a mass movement.

REFLECTIONS

1. Anabaptists, Congregationalists, Baptists, Quakers, Unitarians, and Methodists are enormously diverse. What do they have in common?
2. How do Lutheran, Calvinist, and Anglican churches compare with Nonconformist churches? What are other differences between the two groups?

---

18. Noll, "John Wesley," 161.
19. Catterall, "Distinctiveness of British Socialism," 131, 152.
20. Wesley, "Sermon 22," Discourse 2.III.18.

3. How do Nonconformists treat the Sermon on the Mount? What can we learn from Anabaptists, Quakers, and John Wesley? How can each tradition encourage us in our discipleship?

4. It has been argued that British socialism owes more to Methodism/Nonconformity than it does to Marxism. What might this mean? What questions do you have about this assertion?

Prayer Thought

Loving God, help me be courageous, patient, and true to your ways, and righteousness. Help me learn from Christians who are willing to be "nonconformists." Amen.

26

Colonizing Times

Exporting Christendom in European Empires

The first major European empires were Catholic, Spanish, and Portuguese, begun after Christopher Columbus sailed across the Atlantic looking for a way to India, "discovering" the Americas in 1492. Thus begins the story of how European Christendom was exported from Europe, first Catholic, and later Protestant.

An early memory for me was my mother showing me a world atlas and pointing out all the countries in red, those which were part of the British Empire. I sensed British importance on the world stage. We were number one. When I was sixteen or seventeen, I read about the British/China Opium Wars, 1839–42 and 1856–60. To foster the drug trade of the British East India Company, Britain forced China to import opium. China resisted and lost. These stories upended forever my naive view of the British Empire as a good thing. More recent reading has not changed my opinion. Opium was the third-highest moneymaker for British India, after land and salt. Thomas Manuel asserts, "The British Raj in the nineteenth century was a narco-state, a country sustained by trade in an illegal drug."[1]

There is another story from my mother. Through her mother, Winifred, she was related to the Tucker family, a family of professional watercolor artists who settled in the English Lake District in 1865. Edward and Julia Tucker were watercolor artists who had five sons, who themselves became

---

1. Cited in Sanghera, *Empireworld*, 9.

watercolor artists. I have some of their wonderful pictures in the room in which I am writing this chapter.

The five brothers set a Lake District walking record in June 1877. They climbed four of the highest mountains in the Lake District and England, and walked sixty-five miles in nineteen hours and thirty-eight minutes—a record that stood until 1895.[2] They all played football for Ambleside, and Arthur was also captain of the Windermere cricket team.[3] Not only were they artists, they were also athletes. One of them, Alfred, became an Anglican bishop in Africa. He was an artist, an athlete, and a bishop.

Bishop Tucker first became Anglican bishop of Eastern Equatorial Africa in 1890. In this role, he was the third bishop; the first bishop had been murdered, and the second bishop had died of fever on his way to Uganda. On Tucker's first mission trip, he walked 800 miles from Mombasa on the coast to Mengo, a part of Kampala in Uganda. He walked this journey back and forth several times, and is reputed to have been called the "Uganda Express." He later became the first Anglican bishop of Uganda.

He arrived in Uganda in December of 1890, to find a civil war in progress. In 1892 there was a further crisis; the Imperial British East Africa Company (IBEAC) had decided to withdraw, because the British government had not introduced a railway as promised. In response, Tucker campaigned for Uganda to become a British colony, and this happened in 1894. The Church Missionary Society also funded IBEAC, to enable it to stay in Uganda.[4] His logic was that colonization would end the religious wars in the country and ensure the survival of the Anglican church. At the same time, Tucker successfully implemented a strong vision of indigenous African church leadership. Was Tucker nevertheless a British imperialist, an agent of expanding Anglican Christendom? Or was he both, caught in British imperial times, but sometimes subversive?

The following picture in the London Illustrated News in 1890 is interesting:

---

2. Palmer, *In Lakeland Dells and Fells*, 67–68.
3. Shepherd, *Tucker of Uganda*, 18.
4 Byaruhanga, *Bishop Alfred Robert Tucker*, 36.

Part Three | Living the Sermon on the Mount in Difficult Times

Here we have Bishop Tucker, as the new bishop of East Equatorial Africa, on the same page with two British soldiers. What does this imply?

Sri Lankan theologian Aloysius Pieris has called merchant, missionary, and military "an unholy alliance."[5] They match the three temptations of Jesus: economic power, religious institutional power, and military power.[6] The Roman Empire depended on all three, as did the British Empire. There is the profit motive, the seduction of religious ideology justifying takeover, and military might to enforce domination. Empire cannot happen without all three engaged. This above page from the *London Illustrated News* is doubly strong on militarism, but the Imperial British East Africa Company is in the background in the Uganda story.

However, Tucker was an evangelical Anglican adult convert, and his soulmate Josephine was a Quaker. He began as a working artist with irregular income. Later he was a champion of the Ugandan church becoming an indigenous self-supporting, self-propagating, and self-governing body.[7] Joan Mattia suggests after reading Tucker's frank and intimate letters and looking at the portrayal of Africans in his artwork, that Tucker was perhaps

---

5. Cited in Rajkumar, "Postcolonialism and Re-stor(y)ing," 104.
6. Matthew 4:1–11.
7. Byaruhanga, *Bishop Alfred Robert Tucker*, 13, 14, 16.

more in loyal opposition to British colonialism than abetting it. He was more prophet than chaplain to British imperialists.[8]

It is helpful to summarize the British Empire. At its height, between World War I and II, it covered a quarter of the globe. It ruled 500 million people, a fifth of the world's population. Politically, economically, and in terms of strategic reach, it was the world's single superpower. Ashley Jackson states, "The Empire was a product of the rise of global capitalism, an international order underwritten by Britain, until replaced by America in the twentieth century."[9]

Sathnam Sanghera writes splendid, critical, nuanced, and fair accounts of the British Empire, but he still upsets British patriots.[10] However, history is clear. Twelve and a half million Africans were victims of the slave trade, with three million transported by the British.[11] Plantation capitalism provided industrial capitalism and expanding consumerism with cheap products like sugar and cotton, and later in India and Malaya, tea and rubber.[12] Slavery and sugar made Barbados one of the richest and most brutal places in the Americas.[13] Indigenous people in the Americas were without immunity to European diseases, and this made it easier for white settler colonizers to rob land in the Americas.[14] White settler colonialism also thrived in Australia, New Zealand, South Africa and elsewhere in Africa, and ... in Palestine.[15]

Atlantic slavery is a big issue. The port of Liverpool, England, did very well out of slavery. However, one cannot go through Liverpool's International Slavery Museum and come out thinking slavery was a good thing.

Slavery was abolished in the British Empire in 1833, through the efforts of William Wilberforce, other evangelicals, and Quakers, aided by slave rebellions. Indentured labor from India replaced slavery in many places.[16]

---

8. Mattia, *Walking the Rift*.
9. Jackson, *British Empire*, 9.
10. Sanghera, *Empireworld*, 19–20.
11. Sanghera, *Empireworld*, 86.
12. Sanghera, *Empireworld*, 21.
13. Sanghera, *Empireworld*, 29.
14. Sanghera, *Empireworld*, 22.
15. For a critical Israeli perspective on settler colonialism in Palestine, see Halper, *Decolonizing Israel, Liberating Palestine*, 17–111.
16. Sanghera, *Empireworld*, chapter 3.

Part Three | Living the Sermon on the Mount in Difficult Times

Famine lurked frequently in the British Empire. A million died in the Irish potato famine in the 1840s, and in the last quarter of the nineteenth century, India suffered twenty-four famines, and this pressurized some Indians to risk indentured labor.[17] The last major famine in India was the Bengal famine in 1942–44, in which, conservatively, around three million people died.[18] As Indian economist and Nobel Prize winner Amartya Sen has observed, since independence there has not been a famine in India.[19]

British justice in India and elsewhere was about white supremacy. In 1907, the Indian nationalist Bal Gangadhar Tilak stated, "The goddess of British Justice, though blind, is able to distinguish unmistakably black from white."[20]

Some countries are unstable and violent today as a result of their British colonial history: Nigeria, Kashmir, Burma/Myanmar, Iraq, Sudan, Eritrea, and Palestine.[21]

The debate about the British Empire continues, but the Bible is not neutral. God was on the side of slaves in Egypt. In Matthew's Gospel, we have the final judgement of the nations parable in which Jesus gives us his criteria for evaluating empires and nations:

> Come, you that are blessed by my Father, inherit the kingdom prepared for you from the foundation of the world; for I was hungry and you gave me food, I was thirsty and you gave me something to drink, I was a stranger and you welcomed me, I was naked and you gave me clothing, I was sick and you took care of me, I was in prison and you visited me.[22]

Was the British Empire a good thing? We should measure it by Jesus' criteria above, and also ask the opinions of black and brown people, descendants of victims of European empires. We should privilege the voices of the children of slaves.

Black and brown lives matter!

We also need to address the problem of whiteness as a way of systematically privileging white people, socially, economically, and politically, through violence, occupation, discrimination, and supremacy. Miguel Da

---

17. Sanghera, *Empireworld*, 84–85.
18. Puri, "Three Million."
19. Myhrvold-Hanssen, "Democracy, News Media, and Famine Prevention."
20. Sanghera, *Empireworld*, 166.
21. Sanghera, *Empireworld*, 211–15.
22. Matthew 25:31–45.

La Torre writes, "For white privilege to be maintained, white ignorance must be sustained."[23] As a white person, I thus need to understand current and historical racism, including colonialism. Critical race theory is helpful in questioning and unpacking whiteness.[24]

We next turn to see how the Sermon on the Mount was used in strategies of liberation.

REFLECTIONS

1. Look again at the side-by-side portraits of Bishop Tucker, Captain Younghusband, and Colonel Hayter. To what extent might Anglican Bishop Tucker have been compromised by British colonialism in his Christian witness and service in Uganda?
2. How do we deal with compromised Christianity in European and American colonialism?
3. According to Oxfam, in the US the wealth of a typical black household is just 15.8 percent of that of a typical white household.[25] Should Christians be pressing for financial reparations for the descendants of African slaves as justice and for reconciliation?
4. "Black Lives Matter!" Why for some people is this controversial?
5. Is "Love your neighbor as yourself" a way of navigating culture wars in Britain, the US, and elsewhere?

Prayer Thought

Loving Parent of all, your son grew up and lived in a colonized land. He knew the story of your enslaved people in Egypt and that you led them to a promised land of equality, milk, and honey. Help us work for your kingdom on earth today. Amen.

---

23. Miguel Da La Torre, cited in Cruchley, "Turning Whiteness Purple," 256.
24. Delgado and Stefancic, *Critical Race Theory*.
25. Riddell et al., "Inequality Inc.," 5.

27

Freedom Times

Gandhi, King, and Chávez

The role of British Nonconformist Christianity in the rise of British socialism has already been mentioned. After the Labour Party's victory in 1945, this led to the introduction of the welfare state, including the National Health Service. It was the same Labour government that facilitated Indian independence in 1947.

We are now going to look at exodus from empire and oppression Jesus-style. We will see how the Sermon on the Mount was core to a) Gandhi's campaigns for independence in India; b) the American civil rights movement led within black churches with Martin Luther King Jr.; and c) the work of César Chávez as a union organizer among Filipino and Mexican farm workers in California.

FREEDOM TIMES: MAHATMA GANDHI, INDIA

It was a vegetarian Christian from Manchester that gave eighteen-year-old Mohandas K. Gandhi a copy of the Bible around 1888, when Gandhi was a student studying law in London. He said the Sermon on the Mount "went straight to my heart . . . left a deep impression on my mind when I read it . . . delighted me beyond measure . . . gave me comfort and boundless joy."[1] Gandhi went on to read the Sermon on the Mount every day for forty years.[2]

Gandhi found that taking this message of Jesus to practice wholehearted generosity with your enemies was also a way of disarming them.

It was when he first went to South Africa in 1893, as a lawyer serving the Indian community, that the revolutionary political philosophy of *Satyagraha* (truth force, nonviolent civil resistance) was birthed. It was a way of resisting British colonial racism and oppression.

Gandhi believed that Jesus meant the Sermon on the Mount to be lived by everyone, not just the first apostles, and he sought to demonstrate this in his life and campaigns in South Africa, and later in India. He insisted the Sermon on the Mount was to be taken seriously. He found to his surprise and dismay that most British Christians ignored the Sermon on the Mount. They thought it an impossible ideal, not meant for living in the real world. In contrast, Gandhi thought the Sermon on the Mount was given not just for peaceful disciples, but above all to a groaning world.[3]

Gandhi's genius was this. As a trained lawyer, he began with his respect for law, but distinguished between just and unjust laws. He broke unjust laws creatively, strategically, and at the same time, did not avoid arrest or imprisonment. His disobedience was thus civil, not criminal. Combining respect for law, yet breaking unjust, oppressive laws in the spirit of the Sermon on the Mount gave his resistance to British colonialism an ethical and effective edge. He seized the higher moral ground, and this created favorable publicity in newspapers for the cause of Indian independence. At the same time, he was always respectful in his attitude to British colonial officials. He humanized the conflict. Finally, he led millions in massive civil disobedience campaigns. The Salt March in 1930 was one of the most famous and effective protests.

Oppressed peoples are likely to lose most violent conflicts. It is an unequal contest in a colonial struggle. The poor did not have the money, weapons, training, or organization that their European oppressors had. However, the Sermon on the Mount gave Gandhi a new way for oppressed Indians to creatively resist, and millions marched in massive, nonviolent civil disobedience campaigns. India became ungovernable for the British.

---

1. Subrahmanyan, "Mahatma Gandhi," 3, 2.
2. Dennis, ed., *Choosing Peace*, 136.
3. Subrahmanyan, "Mahatma Gandhi," 5.

Part Three | Living the Sermon on the Mount in Difficult Times

India finally became independent in 1947, although not without many tragedies, including the violent partition of greater India into Muslim Pakistan and an India with a Hindu majority, but set up with a secular constitution. India is the largest democracy in the world. Gandhi was assassinated by Hindu nationalist Nathuram Godse, when going to prayer on January 30, 1948.

FREEDOM TIMES: THE US CIVIL RIGHTS MOVEMENT

> To our most bitter opponents we say: "We will match your capacity to inflict suffering by our capacity to endure suffering. We will meet your physical force with soul force. Do to us as you will, and we shall continue to love you. We cannot in all good conscience obey your unjust laws because non-co-operation with evil is as much a moral obligation as is co-operation with good. Throw us in jail, and we shall still love you. Send your hooded perpetrators of violence into our community at the midnight hour and beat us and leave us half dead, and we shall still love. But be ye assured that we will wear you down by our capacity to suffer. One day we shall win freedom, but not only for ourselves. We shall so appeal to your heart and conscience that we shall win *you* in the process, and our victory will be a double victory. (Martin Luther King Jr.)[4]

Blacks in the US have suffered tragically through slavery, segregation, being deprived of voting rights, trapped in poverty, employment discrimination, suffering inferior schooling, beaten, harassed, framed, lynched, bombed, shot, and terrorized. When a Christian black woman named Rosa Parks refused with dignity to give up her seat on a Montgomery, Alabama bus on December 1, 1955, her simple act of resistance started the US civil rights movement. For 383 days, blacks in Montgomery refused to use the public bus system, until the Supreme Court ruled that segregated transportation was unconstitutional. An unknown twenty-six-year-old black minister was the spokesperson for the boycott. His name was Dr. Martin Luther King Jr. He became spokesperson for the ongoing civil rights movement, "a drum major for justice,"[5] to use his term. The civil rights movement grew out of the black churches, informed by both suffering and the Bible, following

---

4. King Jr., *Strength to Love*, 54–55.
5. King Jr., "Drum Major Instinct Speech."

the Jesus who was also lynched, but who stood in the exodus tradition of freeing people from slavery.

The courage of those who were beaten, spit on, and tear-gassed, but did not retaliate as they protested, won the hearts and minds of millions to the civil rights cause. Lunch counter sit-ins, Freedom Rides, voter registration, the March on Washington, the Selma to Montgomery March, police dogs and firehoses set on demonstrators in Birmingham, Alabama, all changed public opinion. They made visible to a wider public the injustices and humiliations blacks were suffering every day. Millions marched, black and white, Catholic, Protestant, and Jewish, young and old. They sang, "We shall overcome..."

King's "Letter from a Birmingham Jail"[6] almost belongs in the New Testament—such is its prophetic spirit, power, and clarity about nonviolently disobeying unjust laws. King also spoke out courageously and forcefully about the Vietnam War, angering President Lyndon Johnson, but resisting American empire. The Poor People's March on Washington, DC in 1968 was for economic justice and human rights for all poor people. King, still a young man, was assassinated by a sniper's bullet on April 4, 1968.

A series of acts ran through the US Congress and were signed into law by President Johnson from 1964 to 1968, ending segregation.

The US civil rights movement began with a dream of justice and equality, the biblical promised land. By refusing to give up her bus seat in Montgomery, Alabama on December 1, 1955, Rosa Parks was demonstrating the last and hardest Beatitude, "Blessed are those who are persecuted for justice/righteousness' sake, for theirs is the kingdom of heaven."[7] She had trained in nonviolent resistance, and was part of a well worked-out strategy. She was a member of the African Methodist Episcopal Church all her life.

FREEDOM TIMES: CÉSAR E. CHÁVEZ AND FARM WORKERS

César Chávez (1927–1993) was born in Arizona into a Mexican-American Catholic family. He grew up to become a labor leader and civil rights activist committed to nonviolent methods. Chávez and Dolores Huerta co-founded what became the United Farm Workers (UFW) labor union in

6. King, "'Negro Is Your Brother,'" 80.
7. Matthew 5:10–11.

Part Three | Living the Sermon on the Mount in Difficult Times

1967. An early success was organizing the Delano grape strikes 1965–1970, which included a consumer boycott of table grapes until a fair deal for farm workers was achieved. I was in California in the summer of 1969 picking raisin grapes, which were not part of the grape boycott. I slept in a tractor shed. My fellow field workers were kind, skilled, and could pick grapes much faster than me. I was astonished at the attitude of the Anglo foreman who, while treating me with dignity, just saw other farm workers as another thing like machinery, fertilizer, and so on. I had not met such dehumanizing attitudes before, growing up in farming communities in the North of England.

How did Chávez live out the Sermon on the Mount? It was in his commitment to justice for farm workers, and his uncompromising use of nonviolent methods in "La Causa"—union organizing and actions for justice. He walked the Beatitudes. He knew poverty of spirit and hungered for justice. In his commitment to nonviolence, he was rich in mercy. He knew what it was to be harassed for standing up for what was right. He believed that, in time, the determined meek would indeed inherit the earth. The Beatitudes were actually his favorite passage of Scripture:

> [The Beatitudes] embody both charity and justice; and they speak directly to Christ's central message, which is "Love thy neighbour." We're doing Christ's work on earth; and we're reminded ever so much in the Beatitudes of what it is he wanted us to do: the thing about loving him and loving our neighbour.[8]

Chávez left school at the age of fourteen, and so did not go to university. Nevertheless, Jose-Antonio Orosco argues that Chávez "was a sophisticated thinker, who through the course of his activism, reflected carefully on the nature of nonviolence and American society and sought to understand the conditions for bringing about social change in the United States."[9]

Chávez was rooted deeply in Christian experience.[10] When I talked with the daughter of Dolores Huerta, she told of her experiences as a child, of how the union workers and their families lived close together, shared in Mass and prayers as well as union organizing. Chávez was mentored in the 1950s by Father Donald McDonnell, a parish priest and labor organizer, who introduced him to Catholic social teaching, St. Francis, and Gandhi.

---

8. Cited in García, *Gospel of César E. Chávez*, 126.
9. Orosco, *Cesar Chavez*, 5.
10. García, *Gospel of César Chávez*, 1–23.

HOW SUCCESSFUL HAS NONVIOLENCE BEEN IN THE TWENTIETH CENTURY?

Are these freedom movements exceptions? Erica Chenoweth observes, "The horrors of war have become much more visible than in the past, while realistic alternatives are more clearly within reach."[11] With others, Chenoweth's research on violent and nonviolent conflicts since 1900 can be summarized as follows:

> Among the 565 campaigns that have both begun and ended over the past 120 years, about 51 percent of the nonviolent campaigns have succeeded outright, while only about 26 percent of the violent ones have. Nonviolent resistance thus outperforms violence by a 2-to-1 margin. (Sixteen percent of the nonviolent campaigns and 12 percent of violent ones ended in limited success, while 33 percent of nonviolent campaigns and 61 percent of violent ones ultimately failed.) Moreover, in countries where civil-resistance campaigns took place, chances of democratic consolidation, periods of relative post-conflict stability, and various quality-of-life indicators were higher after the conflict than in the countries that experienced civil war.[12]

Thus, Gandhi and the Indian independence movement, the American civil rights movement, and Chávez's union organizing are not exceptions, but the rule. The spirit and creative practice of the Sermon on Mount can be liberational, ways of doing exodus Jesus-style, for oppressed peoples suffering in empire from white supremacy.

REFLECTIONS

1. Which stories in this chapter stand out for you? Which for you are the most moving?
2. What can we learn about Sermon on the Mount discipleship from these stories? Is the Sermon on the Mount a realistic way of working against injustice, or is it too idealistic and naive about the real world?

---

11. Chenoweth, "Future of Nonviolent Resistance," 72.

12. Chenoweth, "Future of Nonviolent Resistance," 74. See also Chenoweth and Stephan, *Why Civil Resistance Works*.

Part Three | Living the Sermon on the Mount in Difficult Times

3. What is your response to the work of Erica Chenoweth and others that nonviolent campaigns are more effective than violent ones in changing governments, improving human rights, and establishing democracies in the last 120 years?

Prayer Thought

Loving God, thank you for stories of discipleship courage. May I learn from them and act with the same courage, wisdom, and skill. Amen.

28

World War I Times

The War to End All Wars?

THE TRAGEDY

"The First World War was a tragic and unnecessary conflict..." are the first and poignant words of British military historian John Keegan in his book *The First World War*.[1] Keegan is not alone in this assessment. Other historians, both left and right, now see World War I (WWI) as a terrible mistake.[2]

Gavrilo Princip, a nineteen-year-old Bosnian Serb nationalist, shot Archduke Franz Ferdinand and his wife, Sophie, in Sarajevo on June 28, 1914. How did this trigger WWI?

There had been no major war in Europe since Waterloo and the defeat of Napoleon Bonaparte in 1815—a hundred years of peace. Norman Angell argued just before WWI broke out that war was in no one's interests in modern global capitalism. Thus, war was either unlikely or would be brief.[3] His book was very popular, but events proved Angell wrong—he underestimated nationalism.

Nationalisms were surging[4] with increasing rivalries between European empires, the Ottoman Empire, and also rising Japan. Germany after 1870 became a newly formed united nation, and had imperial ambitions of

1. Keegan, *First World War*, 3.
2. Clinton, "War against War," 485.
3. Angell, *Great Illusion*.
4. For a nuanced treatment of nationalism, 1870–1918, see Hobsbawn, *Nations and Nationalism Since 1780*, chapter 4.

its own. A naval arms race began as Germany sought to rival Britain's navy and end its naval dominance. Sides began to form from 1907 with Russia, France, and Britain on one side, and Germany and Austria-Hungary on the other. All were empires, or as in Germany's case, wanted to become an empire. Yet no one dreamed a world war was about to begin in the summer of 1914. Cambridge historian Christopher Clark concludes his book on the origins of WWI with these awful words: "the protagonists of 1914 were sleepwalkers watchful but unseeing, haunted by dreams, yet blind to the reality of the horror they were about to bring into the world."[5]

Matthew Naylor, CEO of the US WWI Museum in Kansas City, Missouri, calls WWI the "founding catastrophe of the twentieth century."[6] Who was responsible? Sandi Cooper points out that WWI was "unleashed by anywhere between fourteen and forty-five men."[7]

After pursuing an initial policy of neutrality under President Wilson, the US entered WWI on April 6, 1917. Ironically, it was also Good Friday. Promised by President Wilson as the war to end all wars, WWI actually created massively more violence in its widening turbulence in the twentieth century. WWI contributed to the Arminian genocide, the Bolshevik Revolution in 1917, Irish independence in 1921, the rise of Mussolini and Hitler's fascism, WWII (1939–45), the Holocaust, and the Cold War (1946–1989). With nuclear weapons we have moved from the Arminian genocide in WWI to the possibility of omnicide, the death of all of us.

The slogan "war to end all wars" was a terrible illusion.

Ultimately WWI resulted in over 8.5 million military deaths, and between 6.6 and 13 million civilian deaths.[8] Made worse by the war, the Spanish flu epidemic in 1918–1919 killed between 17 and 100 million people.[9] WWI ended empires, added to others, and redrew maps, beginning in Europe. The maps redrawn in the Middle East still plague us with consequences today. The 9/11 attack in 2001 is one of those consequences, when

---

5. Clark, *Sleepwalkers*, 562.

6. Naylor, introductory speech to a conference "Remembering Muted Voices: Conscience, Dissent, Resistance, and Civil Liberties in World War I through Today." National World War I Museum and Memorial, Kansas City, Missouri, October 19, 2017.

7. Cooper, "Book Review," 577.

8. "Source List and Detailed Death Tolls for the Primary Megadeaths of the Twentieth Century." There is a consensus of around 8.5 million military deaths. Civilian death estimates range from 6.6 million to 13 million, depending on whether the Russian Civil War and the Arminian massacres are included.

9. Roser, "Spanish Flu."

hijacked airplanes crashed into the Twin Towers in New York, the Pentagon in Washington, DC, and in Pennsylvania. The continuing conflicts in the Middle East, including Israel/Palestine, are consequences of WWI.

RESISTANCE TO WORLD WAR I

> The climax [of British censorship in WWI] was reached, however, when 20,000 copies of the Sermon on the Mount (printed without comment as a leaflet) were ordered by a magistrate in Leeds to be destroyed as seditious literature, and their would-be distributor was committed to jail under a sentence of three months hard labour. The War Office and the Bench knew, if the Church did not, that war and the Sermon on the Mount could not co-exist.[10]

Why did WWI happen in Christendom Europe? The gods of nationalism and imperialism were worshipped instead of the humble Nazarene who taught the Sermon on the Mount. Pope Benedict XV, pope from 1914 to 1922, called WWI "the suicide of civilized Europe" and worked hard, but unsuccessfully, for peace.[11] Thus, Catholics shot Catholics, and Protestants bayoneted Protestants. Many priests, bishops, pastors, and preachers abandoned the Sermon on the Mount to preach religious nationalism.

David Lloyd George, British Secretary of State for War and later wartime Prime Minister, wanted to make the path for conscientious objectors (COs) "a very hard one," even though conscientious objection was legal.[12] Around forty COs were taken to France to be shot, and were only saved by the intervention of Quaker members of parliament. The torture treatment of being tied to a stake was used. It was called crucifixion. Prison conditions were harsh, with insufficient food. Seventy-three British COs died either in prison or as a direct result of their incarceration. Thirty-one went insane from their treatment.[13]

---

10. Richards, *Christian's Alternative to War*, 89.

11. Wikipedia, "Pope Benedict XV."

12. David Lloyd George, Secretary of State for War, July 26, 1916, cited in Boulton, *Objection Overruled*, 10.

13. Boulton, *Objection Overruled*, 11. See 266 for a list of names of the seventy-three who died. For a longer discussion of those who went insane, see 258.

Part Three | Living the Sermon on the Mount in Difficult Times

Cyril Pearce is a meticulously thorough historian and has written a great book on conscientious objectors in WWI.[14] His data base of around 20,000 people is the foundation of his research. He tells wonderful stories of communities resisting, with socialists, nonconformist Christians, and radical suffragist/suffragette women working together to support COs and their families.

Pearce helpfully structures his book to survey patterns of dissent in Birmingham, London, and Scotland. He looks at "hot spots" in Bristol, Croydon, Letchworth, Aberavon, and Briton Ferry, and reviews what he calls "heartlands" in Lancashire, Middlesex, and the West Riding of Yorkshire.

What do we learn from Cyril Pearce and WWI that is relevant for today? In grassroots communities there can be significant resistance to war and injustice. There were many who rejected the sins of nationalism, capitalism, and empire. Pearce reminds us of the importance of belonging to a progressive peace group, working with allies even if you have differences, together creating communities of resistance that support those willing to be at the forefront for justice and peace. We still need COs against war, but also objectors to practices leading to poverty, neoliberal economics, climate change, racism, sexism, and fascism. Many outside the church can catch the spirit and practice of the Sermon on the Mount.

If Cyril Pearce gives a splendid overview of conscientious objection in Britain, Clive Barrett's marvelously written book *Subversive Peacemakers* is also excellent in dealing with the Church of England's story in WWI.[15] Barrett's book is a robust prophetic criticism of the Church of England in WWI as it continued the long-established trinity of power: government, military, and church. Barrett writes as an Anglican priest, and he is searingly critical of warmongering bishops and priests, for example the bellicose bishops of London and Liverpool, and the Anglican vicar in Sutton who opposed every argument of conscience as he served on the local tribunal judging COs. At the same time, Barrett writes about subversive Anglican resisters to war, for example preacher and suffragist Maude Royden, Labour political leader George Lansbury, friend of Gandhi Charles Freer Andrews, and founder of the Peace Pledge Union, Dick Sheppard. Anglican COs were a tiny minority,[16] but those Anglicans who did resist are inspiring.

14. Pearce, *Communities of Resistance*.
15. Barrett, *Subversive Peacemakers*.
16. Barrett, *Subversive Peacemakers*, 119, 122.

Despite all the propaganda coming from Anglican clergy in support of the war, "It was left to the fighting men to realize that the religion of Christ is incompatible with the brutal strategy of modern warfare . . . The soldiers knew only too well that it was not God's war they were fighting."[17] Barrett summarizes the result in these words, "The Church was in the process of losing a gender and a generation, but could not see it."[18]

The US's entrance was decisive. As in the UK, conscientious objection was a legal option in the USA, but difficult. The story of four Hutterites, spiritual cousins of the Amish and Mennonites, has been well documented.[19] At Fort Leavenworth, Kansas, two of the four, brothers Joseph and Michael Hofer, died from their earlier savage treatment at Alcatraz, California. The Hofer brothers were married, with young families, and they were farmers. They belonged to an Anabaptist communal tradition going back 400 years, during which time none had committed murder, and none had served in the military. In their communal life there was no poverty and they did not need police.

It was ironic that they died because they refused to compromise the Sermon the Mount, and lived a Christian life of communal peace and justice. In total, at least twenty-nine COs died in the US. Seventeen out of the twenty-nine who died were members of the Anabaptist family (Hutterites, Mennonites, Amish, Brethren). Out of nearly 600 COs who were held at Fort Leavenworth, sixteen died.[20] Hutterite colonies in the US, traumatized by the treatment of the Hofer brothers and over sixty other Hutterite COs, moved to Canada. Mennonites and others refusing to buy war bonds were also persecuted for their stand.

Sometimes it is argued that the freedom of COs to resist came from the courage of those who served in the military and fought for democracy. The opposite is true. Most militaries were used by the rich and powerful to prevent the development of democracy. The militaries of all countries brutally repressed COs in WWI. It was the suffering of COs that won the right to conscientiously object through advocacy by civil liberties organizations. In the UK, it was through the work of the National Council for Civil

---

17. Barrett, *Subversive Peacemakers*, 173.
18. Barrett, *Subversive Peacemakers*, 173.
19. Stoltzfus, *Pacifists in Chains*.
20. Yoder, "World War I Conscientious Objector Data Base."

Liberties,[21] and in the USA, this is how the American Civil Liberties Union (ACLU) was born—defending COs in WWI.[22]

Others resisted in WWI, including suffragettes. Many unknown soldiers refused to fire, or fired not to kill. Soldier poets like Wilford Owen and Siegfried Sassoon told the damning truth in brief, well-crafted poetic verse. In all this resistance, COs have been called the shock troops of dissent.[23]

Finally, it should be remembered that Keir Hardie, the first British Labour Party Member of Parliament, and its first party leader, was a Christian lay preacher and a pacifist, as well as a socialist. Anglican George Lansbury was also a Christian pacifist, socialist, campaigner for the right for women to vote, and a future Labour Party leader. Both Keir Hardie and George Lansbury campaigned against WWI, even though they were jeered at and mocked for their stand.

The Versailles Peace Treaty in 1919 was very unjust to Germany; it was an act of retaliation and created the conditions for the rise of Hitler and WWII.

REFLECTIONS

1. What do you think about WWI? Was it a crime, a tragedy, or a just war?
2. One of the slogans of WWI was that it was a war to end all wars. In hindsight has that been true? Does war end war?
3. In WWI would you have voluntarily enlisted, been willing to be drafted/conscripted, or would you have been a conscientious objector?
4. Should the right to be a conscientious objector be a human right? Is military conscription or the draft a form of slavery?
5. When we look back at WWI, who was on the right side of history?

---

21. Boulton, *Objection Overruled*, 119. Another civil liberties organization also called the National Council for Civil Liberties was founded in 1934, and it should not be confused with the organization that worked in WWI.

22. The US National Civil Liberties Bureau working for COs in WWI was the forerunner of what became known as the American Civil Liberties Union after the war.

23. Bennett and Howlett, *Antiwar Dissent*, 15.

Prayer Thought

Loving God of all humankind, help us discern what is your will in times of war. Help us in particular learn the ways of your Son. Amen.

29

Nazi Times

Courage in the Terror—Le Chambon and Bonhoeffer

Two hundred thousand US soldiers fought in the Philippines [1899–1902], suffering seven thousand casualties (3.5 percent). Twenty percent of the Philippine population died, mostly civilians, as a result of the US army's scorched-earth strategy (food deprivation, targeting civilians for killing, and so on) and displacement.

—Roxanne Dunbar-Ortiz[1]

We are not a young people with an innocent record and a scanty inheritance. We have engrossed to ourselves ... an altogether disproportionate share of the wealth and traffic of the world. We have got all we want in territory, and our claim to be left in unmolested enjoyment of vast and splendid possessions, mainly acquired by violence, largely maintained by force, often seems less reasonable to others than to us.

—Winston Churchill[2]

---

1. Dunbar-Ortiz, *An Indigenous Peoples' History*, 166.
2. Cited in Megoran, *Warlike Christians in an Age of Violence*, 137–38.

A CRITICAL RE-EVALUATION

The unjust Versailles Treaty in 1919 at the end of World War I (WWI) was a crushing retaliation against Germany. It sowed the seeds for the rise of Hitler and World War II (WWII).

WWII was the most destructive war in history with 40 to 50 million people killed and millions displaced.[3] Nick Megoran, a political geographer at Newcastle University, describes WWII as a war between contending empires, the big seven: Russia, Germany, the United Kingdom, France, USA, Italy, and Japan. He explores how British and Americans see it as a war between goodies and baddies, and how today Anglo-American identity is firmly embedded in the story that the allies were the goodies. Megoran asks, were the British and Americans really goodies in this conflict?[4]

The story of Britain and the US in the nineteenth and twentieth century is often sanitized. Honest history reveals imperial ambitions, exploitive greed, competing empires, and the slaughter of many civilians and indigenous peoples. The two quotes at the beginning of this chapter from Roxanne Dunbar-Ortiz and Winston Churchill both assert American and British imperial violence.

In WWII, the deliberate bombing of civilians in German and Japanese cities culminated with the dropping of atom bombs on Hiroshima and Nagasaki.[5] In Germany, 600,000 civilians were killed,[6] and in Japan 241,000 to 900,000.[7] London School of Economics Professor Mary Kaldor said the Nuremberg War Crimes Tribunal in 1945–46 was victor's justice that ignored the crime of deliberate Allied bombing of civilians. Bombing of civilians therefore has continued with impunity, for instance in Vietnam, Iraq, and recently in Gaza. In addition, mention has already been made of the Bengal famine (1942–44) in British India, in which perhaps 3 million people died.

This does not in any way lessen the evil of the Nazis. Nazi Holocaust victims dreadfully totaled 17 million, including 6 million Jews.[8] Megoran

---

3. Chmielewski, "Casualties of World War II."
4. Megoran, *Warlike Christians in an Age of Violence*, 131–33
5. Book Launch, "Global Activism and Humanitarian Disarmament."
6. World History Encyclopedia, "Allied Bombing of Germany."
7. Wikipedia, "Air Raids on Japan."
8. Wikipedia, "Holocaust Victims."

in two well-written chapters explores further the question, "What about Hitler?"⁹

Were the British and Americans really goodies in WWII? Or does this Anglo-American identity goody myth get in the way of Christians understanding the relevance of the Sermon on the Mount? Matthew's Gospel was written speaking plainly about Roman imperial violence and oppression. Informed by Matthew's Gospel, should we also be equally critical about British, American, and German violence and oppression?

Can we resist Hitler using the Sermon on the Mount? Let us now look at two WWII stories where this happened as examples of what is possible.

LE CHAMBON, FRANCE: ANDRÉ AND MAGDA TROCMÉ

Le Chambon is a small village in the mountains of southern France. During WWII, the villagers, together with their pastor, André Trocmé, and spouse Magda, saved about 5,000 people, two-thirds of whom were Jewish refugees. How did this insignificant village act so decisively to save Jews and others, when elsewhere in France and the rest of Europe most people were eagerly collaborating with the Nazis?

The first key to understanding what happened is to read about the history of the villagers—they had a long history of resistance to Paris. They were Huguenots, that is to say Protestants, a minority, who had known persecution by the rest of Catholic France from the time of the Reformation. Part of their tradition was ignoring French laws when they conflicted with their consciences. So, when the Vichy, the collaborating French government of unoccupied France, passed laws against French Jews, the villagers disobeyed them. Instead of exposing Jews and assisting the police in arresting them, they took them in, and helped them to safety in Switzerland, a 300-kilometer journey.

The second key to understanding what happened in Le Chambon is to look at the character and personality of André Trocmé and the team he led in the village. Trocmé had a French father and a German mother. He grew up bilingual, and although French, he loved his German relatives. However, during WWI, German cruelty in Trocmé's city of Saint-Quentin made it difficult for him to suppress his angry hatred against German soldiers. Then he met his first conscientious objector, albeit in German uniform, who shared his bread with him. This had a big impact on him.

---

9. Megoran, *Warlike Christians in an Age of Violence*, chapters 6 and 7.

Later Trocmé trained to be a Protestant pastor, and married Magda, an Italian. Their first two parishes were in northern industrial France. In their second parish, one of the small groups Trocmé was working with was the Men's Circle. It was in one of their meetings that he had an experience with Jesus and the Sermon on the Mount. He expressed the insight that came to him:

> If Jesus really walked upon the earth, why do we keep treating him as if he were a disembodied, impossibly idealistic ethical theory? If he was a real man, then the Sermon on the Mount was made for people on this earth; and if he existed, God has shown us in flesh and blood what goodness is for flesh-and-blood people.[10]

This conviction that the Sermon on the Mount was made for real people on this earth empowered him in his ministry in Le Chambon, his next parish. He had been pastor in the village for five years when WWII began.

When the villagers began to hide Jewish refugees, they did so because of their commitment to help strangers in distress. However, they refused to hate the Germans occupying their country. Under Trocmé's leadership they refused to take any kind of revenge against their oppressors. Their loving nonviolence won them friends among the German and French authorities. Often the night before a raid on the village, the telephone would ring with a brief, anonymous message: "Raid tomorrow." Forewarned, the villagers would hide vulnerable refugees in safety until the raid was over.

Le Chambon has been described as the safest place in all of occupied Europe for Jews. It has also been called a conspiracy of goodness.[11]

DIETRICH BONHOEFFER

Dietrich Bonhoeffer (1906–1945) was a German theologian, a leader in the Confessing Church with Karl Barth and others, who understood early in the 1930s the nature and threat of Nazism. He was arrested by the Gestapo at his parent's home on April 5, 1943, and two years later was executed by hanging at Flossenburg concentration camp on April 9, 1945, just a few days before it was liberated by Allied troops.

10. Hallie, *Lest Innocent Blood*, 68.
11. See *Weapons of the Spirit*—a documentary by Pierre Sauvage, 1989. Pierre Sauvage was born from Jewish parents in the village of Le Chambon, but did not discover the story of what happened there until he was eighteen. A remastered widescreen edition of the film was released in 2024.

Part Three | Living the Sermon on the Mount in Difficult Times

Perhaps Bonhoeffer's most famous book, written in the context of Nazism in Germany, was *Nachfolger* (Discipleship), first published in 1937. In English the book was first published as *The Cost of Discipleship*.[12] Bonhoeffer, page after page, takes the Sermon on the Mount simply, seriously, compellingly. It is not an option; it is the heart of authentic, genuine discipleship. With a passion Bonhoeffer challenges lazy, lukewarm, unfaithful Christians with a pastor's heart and a prophet's soul. I hear Jesus in his words.

The book is also a prophetic criticism of National Socialism and its leader, Hitler. It is a wonder the book was published at all in Nazi Germany. *The Cost of Discipleship* is also for our time, as we suffer authoritarian, racist, populist, and anti-democratic leaders, in Europe, Asia, and the Americas. It is a stinging rebuke to members of the American Christian right.

Everyone agrees that Bonhoeffer was vehemently against Nazism and its antisemitism. However, was his resistance violent or nonviolent? After writing on the Sermon on the Mount in *The Cost of Discipleship*, did Bonhoeffer change his mind, become a realist, and take part in a plot to kill Hitler?

That Bonhoeffer was involved in an assassination plot is the present consensus of most scholars, and is based primarily on the most important biography of Bonhoeffer, written by one of his closest friends, Eberhard Bethge. To overturn this consensus, based on such a credible witness, is a big challenge. But was Bonhoeffer really a potential assassin?

Mark Thiessen Nation argues Bonhoeffer was not. Nation's evidence and arguments are clear and persuasive.[13]

Bonhoeffer was arrested in April 1943, because he was trying to save the lives of fourteen Jews, not because he was involved in a plot to kill the Führer. He was arrested more than a year before the famous assassination attempt on Hitler. The summary of his court proceedings states that Bonhoeffer was sent to prison because he was avoiding military service, and helping others to this end also—he was convicted of being a conscientious objector.[14]

Furthermore, there is clear, written evidence that Bonhoeffer was consistent about Christian nonviolence from sometime before 1933 to the end of his life. Sometime in the period 1940–43 Bonhoeffer wrote his last

---

12. Bonhoeffer, *Cost of Discipleship*.
13. Nation, *Discipleship in a World Full of Nazis*.
14. Nation, *Discipleship in a World Full of Nazis*, 17.

book, *Ethics,* and said this, "The Sermon on the Mount is either valid as the word of God's world-reconciling love everywhere and at all times, or it is not really relevant for us at all."[15] After the war, pre-eminent Protestant theologian Karl Barth, from conversations with Bonhoeffer, said Bonhoeffer "was really a pacifist on the basis of his understanding of the Gospel." When told of Bonhoeffer's possible involvement in an assassination plot, Franz Hildebrandt, Bonhoeffer's "best and most like-minded friend," rejected that idea.[16]

REFLECTIONS

1. Were the British and Americans the goodies in WWII, and the Nazi Germans and the Japanese the baddies? What about the Soviet Union?
2. Does this Anglo-American identity myth about being the goodies in World War II hinder American and British Christians from understanding the Sermon on the Mount as a credible response to empire?
3. If you had lived in the village of Le Chambon in France during WWII, would you have helped refugees, Jewish and others, find their way through the village to safety in Switzerland? What would have been your personal struggles if you had been there?
4. Do you think Bonhoeffer changed his mind about the Sermon on the Mount after he wrote *The Cost of Discipleship*? Was Bonhoeffer part of the plot to assassinate Hitler? What in your mind are the arguments for and against?
5. What can we learn from both the Trocmés and Bonhoeffer about living the Sermon on the Mount in difficult times?

Prayer Thought

Loving God, thank you for the examples of courage given us by those in Le Chambon and by Dietrich Bonhoeffer. Give me grace and insight to really understand your will, and the courage to live it in my difficult times. Amen.

---

15. Nation, *Discipleship in a World Full of Nazis,* 19
16. Nation and Hauerwas, "Pacifist and Enemy of the State."

30

Christian Realism Times
Niebuhr and Hauerwas

REINHOLD NIEBUHR

Reinhold Niebuhr was the theological draftsman of a position called Christian Realism, which has been very influential since WWII. Who was Niebuhr?

Reinhold Niebuhr (1892–1971) was first of all a Reform Protestant pastor in Detroit, Michigan, who had to deal with the inhuman conditions that workers endured in the automobile industry. Although formed by Lutheran theology, "he had all the moral passion and political drive of Calvinism on the prowl."[1] Reinhold Niebuhr addressed political leaders and intellectuals in the US. Informed by the realism of Augustine,[2] the first theological architect of Christendom, Niebuhr enjoyed status as a public theologian on American policy in both WWII and during the Cold War. His dismissal of the Sermon on the Mount was nuanced, as was his embrace of nuclear weapons.[3] He was a sophisticated Christendom theologian, who was also critical of President Nixon having worship services in the White House with the likes of Southern Baptist evangelist Billy Graham.[4]

---

1. Rasmussen, *Reinhold Niebuhr*, 32. Larry Rasmussen was Reinhold Niebuhr professor of social ethics at Union Theological Seminary when he edited this book as a representative selection of Niebuhr's writing, along with a very helpful introduction.

2. Rasmussen, *Reinhold Niebuhr*, 119–26.

3. Sterling, "Reinhold Niebuhr and the Nuclear Dilemma."

4. Rasmussen, *Reinhold Niebuhr*, 269–73.

He changed and adapted his positions with the change of events, new information, and further thinking.

After WWI he was initially a theological liberal, pacifist, and socialist. He later became critical of these positions, and sometimes is placed in the neoorthodox group of theologians together with Karl Barth and Emil Brunner, who were also working after WWI. Niebuhr rejected what he saw as the naivete of theological liberalism, abandoned pacifism, and argued for realism, realism of the world as it is and in its sinfulness. Justice was the nearest we can approach love, yet unconditional agape love judges all attempts at justice and finds them inadequate.[5] He believed that only relative justice was sometimes achievable between groups, and that has to come by force.[6] Notwithstanding Niebuhr's criticism of liberalism, he was more critically liberal than neoorthodox; in fact he did not see himself as neoorthodox.[7] Larry Rasmussen suggests Niebuhr is best described as "Neo-Reformation" in his reworking of Luther and Calvin.[8]

Niebuhr taught at Union Theological Seminary in New York City from 1928 to 1960 and Dietrich Bonhoeffer was one of his students. As an American public theologian, Niebuhr supported WWII, nuclear weapons, and the fight against Communism, although he was against the Vietnam War, and a strong advocate for the American civil rights movement. His perspective was nevertheless largely that of a white American male, and he was criticized by female, black, and "Third World" theologians.[9]

Niebuhr saw the Sermon on the Mount as an "impossible possibility."[10] Sin is so deeply ingrained in people and groups that the Sermon on the Mount is impossible in human history.[11] However, it judges us and rightly provokes guilt that can lead to repentance.[12] For Niebuhr, the Sermon on the Mount will only be possible in the future when Jesus finally comes again. In the meantime, all we can do is work for relative justice and that requires coercion; it has to be fought for.[13] Democracy, although far from perfect, is

---

5. Rasmussen, *Reinhold Niebuhr*, 176–177, 192–212.
6. Rasmussen, *Reinhold Niebuhr*, 53–55.
7. Rasmussen, *Reinhold Niebuhr*, 22.
8. Rasmussen, *Reinhold Niebuhr*, 22–23.
9. Rasmussen, *Reinhold Niebuhr*, 33.
10. Gingerich, "Reinhold Niebuhr," 72.
11. Gingerich, "Reinhold Niebuhr," 72–74, 76.
12. Gingerich, "Reinhold Niebuhr," 80–81.
13. Gingerich, "Reinhold Niebuhr," 80.

Part Three | Living the Sermon on the Mount in Difficult Times

worth defending[14] because it is better than authoritarian governments, like that of Stalin's Communism or Hitler's Nazism.

Niebuhr was criticizing an idealistic and literal view of non-resistance. The context of the phrase, "Do not resist an evildoer" [15] means non-retaliation, and Jesus goes on immediately to describe two creative acts of non-violent resistance that are not retaliatory. Jesus certainly acted in resistance, whether opposing teachings and practices that were dehumanizing, or in turning over the tables of money changers in the temple.

It is interesting that Niebuhr spoke well of Gandhi, who he thought was politically realistic, and understood the need for coercion and pressure, albeit by nonviolent methods.[16] Writing before the American civil rights movement began, he anticipated how black Americans, adopting Gandhian methods, could robustly further their cause.[17] He also praised Quakers, because he thought they assumed political responsibilities, for example they were resisters of evils like slavery, although they disavowed violence.[18] Mennonite pacifism he also saw as valid and not a heresy; their witness of a nonviolent, sharing, unselfish kingdom-of-God life reminds other Christians that relative justice and force are not final ends; sacrificial love is.[19]

One of Niebuhr's big ideas was that human groups (nations, corporations, classes, etc.) were more sinful than individuals.[20] As a realist about sin and groups, Niebuhr was also a realist about power. Justice is only possible through coercive power. Thus, pacifism was naive when faced with ruthless totalitarian regimes like Nazi Germany or Soviet Communism. However, what does one make of Jesus in the realities of Roman colonization, something so ominously evident in the Gospels in particular? And the early Christians seriously lived the Sermon on the Mount for the first 300 years of the church in all the harsh oppressions of the Roman Empire. Elsewhere in this book are stories of many who have taken the Sermon on the Mount seriously in their violent contexts, demonstrating that it is not an impossible possibility.

14. Gingerich, "Reinhold Niebuhr," 79; Rasmussen, *Reinhold Niebuhr*, 250–51.
15. Matthew 5:39.
16. Rasmussen, *Reinhold Niebuhr*, 59–65.
17. Rasmussen, *Reinhold Niebuhr*, 66–67.
18. Rasmussen, *Reinhold Niebuhr*, 73.
19. Rasmussen, *Reinhold Niebuhr*, 238–239.
20. See Niebuhr, *Moral Man and Immoral Society*.

Christian Realism Times

Karl Barth was a leading neoorthodox theologian, and eventually had to leave his teaching post in Nazi Germany to return to Switzerland, yet he was almost a pacifist.[21] In contrast to Barth's European experience of war, perhaps Niebuhr's cultural context of the US made it difficult for him to see beyond the violence of American culture. Violence has worked very successfully for white Americans, and so does Niebuhr reach too readily for more violence? Also, in terms of war, civilian Americans were removed from the horrors that were experienced firsthand by civilians in Europe and Asia. Niebuhr was doing theology from a safe, comfortable place in the most powerful country in the world. Niebuhr spoke more to the powerful in America than to the powerless.[22] Is he an apologist for American military power?[23]

However, Niebuhr's realism about sin and groups is helpful, including the need of oppressed groups to organize for power. Martin Luther King Jr. was influenced and helped by Niebuhr's idea of power. For example, he wrote the following in his famous "Letter from a Birmingham Jail": "Lamentably, it is an historical fact that privileged groups seldom give up their privileges voluntarily. Individuals may see the moral light and voluntarily give up their unjust posture; but, as Reinhold Niebuhr has reminded us, groups tend to be more immoral than individuals."[24]

For Gandhi, Martin Luther King Jr., and Rosa Parks, nonviolent action was a way that ethical power could change the entrenched injustice of colonialism and segregation. Niebuhr felt the only answer to Nazism was war, and to the Soviet Union the threat of war. Niebuhr saw the power of totalitarian regimes as total, monolithic. However, all governments ultimately rule by the consent of the people, no matter how tyrannical,[25] and as political scientist Gene Sharp has pointed out, the political power of any regime is ultimately fragile and vulnerable. "Obedience is at the heart of political power," argues Sharp.[26] Take that away in acts of mass civil disobedience, and the power of tyranny falls. Witness the end of British rule in India, the

---

21. See for instance Borneman, "Barth on War, Peace, and Pacifism."
22. Rasmussen, *Reinhold Niebuhr*, 19.
23. Rasmussen, *Reinhold Niebuhr*, 20.
24. King, "'The Negro Is Your Brother,'" 80.
25. This idea of has a long history beginning with Étienne de La Boétie (1530–63) and his essay "Politics of Obedience: The Discourse of Voluntary Servitude" written in 1550. See also Auguste Comte (1798–1857), the grandfather of sociology, and David Hume (1711–1776) in his "Essay 4: Of the First Principles of Government."
26. Sharp, *Politics of Nonviolent Action*, 16.

fall of Marcos in the Philippines, Pinochet in Chile, and the end of Communism in Eastern Europe.

The fiery Pope Pius XI robustly challenged the Nazi regime in 1937 with the encyclical *Mit brennender Sorge* ("With Burning Worry"), read in every church in the Reich on Palm Sunday 1937.[27] His successor Pope Pius XII fully knew of the savagery of the Nazi invasion of Catholic Poland in 1939, and about the destruction of the Jews.[28] What would have happened if Pope Pius XII had challenged Reich Catholic soldiers that they were fighting an unjust war by unjust means? After all, nearly half of all German/Austrian soldiers were Catholic. It was similar in Italy, where the population was nearly all Catholic. Tragically, Pope Pius XII did not so speak out.[29] In contrast, Catholic leaders later were active in support of bringing down, for instance, President Marcos in the Philippines in 1986.

Mention has already been made of the work of Erica Chenoweth and others, that in the twentieth century, nonviolent resistance was twice as effective as violent resistance, and nonviolent campaigns were also more likely to result in democratic and peaceful societies after a conflict.[30] Niebuhr's reading of the Sermon on the Mount saw it as an impossible possibility. Gandhi, King, and Chávez reading saw it as fully practical for the liberation of their oppressed groups. Let us now turn to Stanley Hauerwas's theological criticism of Niebuhr.

STANLEY HAUERWAS (1940–)

> In short, I want to maintain that the Sermon on the Mount presupposes the existence of a community constituted by the practice of nonviolence and that it is unintelligible divorced from such a community. Or, to put it as contentiously as I can, you cannot rightly read the Sermon on the Mount unless you are a pacifist . . . This means that the Sermon on the Mount obviously makes no sense to those not formed into that body called "church."[31]

---

27. Kertzer, *Pope at War*, 6.
28. Kertzer, *Pope at War*, 472–80 for a summary.
29. Kertzer, *Pope at War*, 472.
30. Chenoweth and Stephan, *Why Civil Resistance Works*, 6–7.
31. Hauerwas, "Living the Proclaimed Reign of God," 153.

Hauerwas taught at Duke University for many years. He is the son of a bricklayer, and was brought up Methodist in Dallas, Texas. Influenced initially by Reinhard and H. Richard Niebuhr, he became critical of their theologies after working for a time with Mennonite John Howard Yoder at the University of Notre Dame.

Hauerwas begins with the reality of the incarnation, which he holds is the true revelation of possibilities in the human situation. Jesus, embodying the Sermon on the Mount, shows us both the love and action of God, and how the kingdom of God is coming into the world. In contrast, Niebuhr begins with history and human reality as it is now. For Niebuhr the Sermon on the Mount is outside history, an impossibility. For Hauerwas, Jesus has fully embodied the Sermon on the Mount in history, and so the "impossible" Sermon on the Mount is possible.[32]

Sermon on the Mount discipleship is only possible by being part of a gathered community around Jesus Christ, the church—"to be saved is to be gathered."[33] The Sermon on the Mount is not a "heroic ethic. It is the constitution of a people."[34] It is only together that the Sermon on the Mount is possible. Not everyone can do all the Sermon on the Mount, but together it can be lived out. The Sermon on the Mount is a gift, not a set of rules. The Sermon on the Mount has to be embodied in the world by the church, as Jesus embodied it. As for the early church, living the Sermon on the Mount was an alternative to the violence of Rome, so the church today has to be an alternative to the violence of our world now.[35]

Mark Gingerich, in his thesis on Niebuhr and Hauerwas and their treatment of the Sermon on the Mount, argues that Hauerwas takes the second person of the Trinity, Jesus, more seriously than Niebuhr. He praises Hauerwas's emphasis on the church as a community. It is church community support that makes living the Sermon on the Mount possible. Gingerich goes one step further—that we also need the power of the Holy Spirit in order to live the Sermon on the Mount together. He concludes insightfully that we need to be fully Trinitarian in order to live out the Sermon on the Mount in the realities of sinful human beings enmeshed in sinful systems of violence.[36]

---

32. Gingerich, "Reinhold Niebuhr," 113–14.
33. Hauerwas, cited in Gingerich, "Reinhold Niebuhr," 92.
34. Hauerwas, cited in Gingerich, "Reinhold Niebuhr," 92.
35. Gingerich, "Reinhold Niebuhr," 92–93.
36. Gingerich, "Reinhold Niebuhr," 104–7.

Part Three | Living the Sermon on the Mount in Difficult Times

It is interesting to speculate how Niebuhr's roots in Calvin and Hauerwas's roots in Wesley influence their different positions on the Sermon on the Mount, notwithstanding the theological sophistication of each of them. Calvin was an expression of Christendom, and Wesley was leaving Christendom, as Methodists became a nonconformist movement. Calvin was pessimistic and supported violence as a necessary evil. Wesley, with his "strange warming of the heart" experience, was more hopeful, and a nonviolent reformer. For Wesley, humans could change through grace and the mutual support of the class meeting. Sanctification in this life was possible. Salvation was both individual and social.

REFLECTIONS

1. Summarize Niebuhr's Christian Realism position. What are its strengths and weaknesses? Do you agree or disagree with it? What reasons can you use for your position?
2. What can we learn from Niebuhr?
3. Christendom theologians (Augustine, Luther, Calvin) lessen the rigor of the Sermon on the Mount and compromise it so rulers can use violence. Non-Christendom thinkers who often suffered the violence of rulers (the early church fathers, monastics, Franciscans, Anabaptists, Quakers, and people like Wesley, Gandhi, King, and Chávez) take the Sermon on the Mount seriously. To which group does a) Niebuhr, or b) Hauerwas belong, and why?

Prayer Thought

Loving God of shalom, what kind of realism are you calling us to in our confusing times? Amen.

31

Now Times

The Possibilities of a New Christian Realism

A NEW CHRISTIAN REALISM

Reinhold Niebuhr's influential Christian Realism belongs in a tradition that begins with Augustine, continues in Christendom, and includes Luther and Calvin. This tradition sees the Sermon on the Mount as nonrealistic in the real world. At the same time, Niebuhr sees Quakers, Gandhi, and the civil rights movement as responsible and realistic while being nonviolent. King, as already mentioned, drew on Niebuhr's analysis that justice only comes through power. For King, Gandhi, and others, this was the power of civil disobedience, massive nonviolent protests, and noncooperation. They were birthing a new kind of Christian Realism more faithful to the Sermon on the Mount.

Can we ask today how realistic Niebuhr's now old Christian Realism is when climate change is humanity's biggest threat, and most conflicts are civil wars in which civilians, women, and children in particular are by far the greatest victims?[1] Many people are more threatened by the rich elites and the security forces of their country than by foreign armies.[2] Old Christian Realism is concerned about the security of the state. Do we need a new Christian Realism with a new model of security that is about people security rather than state security?

---

1. Heathershaw, *Security After Christendom*, 24.
2. Heathershaw, *Security After Christendom*, 179.

Political scientist John Heathershaw, who leans to Anabaptism, suggests a person-centered rather than a state-centered model for a new Christian Realism. He defines security as follows: "Security, or 'the absence of fear,' has three elements: (1) inclusion (who is to be secure); (2) protection (from threats to security), and (3) provision (to live life securely)."[3]

For Heathershaw this means:

1. Inclusion of all, including migrants and refugees. Everyone should be secure.

2. Protection. Protection from violence is the main task of security. According to Johan Galtung, Swedish peace studies pioneer, there are three kinds of violence: (i) personal or direct as in a criminal attack or war; (ii) structural or indirect—like institutions and economic systems, for instance segregation, apartheid, and capitalism; and (iii) cultural justifications for war or structural violence through, for example, religion and ideology.[4] Protection can be nonviolent, for example unarmed civilian accompaniment in civil war contexts. Policing can be unarmed, as in Britain.

3. Provision. Just economics, societal cohesion, and a bearable climate are important in provision. There should be food security, stable employment, and healthcare.

Old Christian Realism supports a Christianity that is in partnership with the powerful and serves their interests. New Christian Realism is for marginal people, who find in the Sermon on the Mount inspiration for nonviolent liberation.

Old Christian Realism was supported by powerful, affluent white men in rich countries. Much of the academic work in international relations has also been carried out by white males. On the other hand, research on nonviolence and its practice is often carried out by women.[5] As already mentioned, Niebuhr was criticized by female, black, and global South theologians.[6] Heathershaw says it is time to decolonize and feminize the debate on security.[7]

---

3. Heathershaw, *Security After Christendom*, 15.
4. Heathershaw, *Security After Christendom*, 251.
5. Heathershaw, *Security After Christendom*, 270–71, 307.
6. Rasmussen, *Reinhold Niebuhr*, 33.
7. Heathershaw, *Security After Christendom*, 307.

Let us now consider briefly two recent major conflicts, the War on Terror after 9/11 and the Ukraine/Russia war.

9/11 AND THE WAR ON TERROR

The terrorist attacks using four civilian airplanes on 9/11 in 2001 resulted in the tragic deaths of nearly 3,000 people. War began in Afghanistan a month later. War was declared against Iraq in 2003, on the pretext it had weapons of mass destruction. None were ever found.

According to the Costs of War Project at Brown University, the wider US-led war on terror, twenty years after 9/11, has cost $8 trillion, with more than 940,000 deaths due to direct war violence, plus an estimated 3.6–3.8 million indirectly, with 432,000 civilians killed. The number of war refugees and displaced persons totals 38 million. At least four times the number of US soldiers killed in combat have sadly died from suicide,[8] with great emotional cost to their families.

American-led revenge for the 3,000 people who tragically died on 9/11 unleashed massive human insecurity for millions of innocent people, while ignoring the crisis of gun deaths, poverty, and police racism at home in the US.

THE UKRAINE AND RUSSIA WAR

This conflict is unusual, because it is a nation-state versus a nation-state war. Most wars today are civil wars. Old Christian Realists would perhaps say that as Hitler needed to be met by force, not appeasement, that is what should happen with President Putin and Russia. Therefore, going to war against an aggressive, invading dictator is the lesser of two evils and the responsible thing to do. Ukraine is clearly fighting a just war.

What might be a Sermon on the Mount Christian perspective in this situation?

John Heathershaw points out many pacifists are neither liberal nor idealist. Mennonite John Howard Yoder, for instance, suggested limited "police action" by the UN could be justified when under international law. So, there are pragmatic and realist pacifist positions.[9] Heathershaw is criti-

---

8. "Costs of War Project."
9. Heathershaw, "Theological Responses to the War against Ukraine," 60.

cal of the just war position. He asserts it is not helpful politically, and lacks faith theologically.[10] He argues for hope, but hope is not pacifist. Rather, hope is "the breaking of Christ into the world to defeat the raging nations and reveal their vanities."[11]

Practically, how would Heathershaw's New Christian Realism address the Ukrainian war? He argues that Unarmed Civilian Protection (UCP), nonviolent resistance, and humanitarian aid by churches and NGOs can create pockets of peace within war. These can be expanded, and create conditions for peace. Mass nonviolent resistance has a participant advantage over armed rebellion, and is twice as effective as violence, according to Chenoweth and Stephan.[12] Nonviolent resistance would not stop an invasion, but it can make it very difficult for an occupying force to govern. The cost of such a conflict in lives, destruction, and economy would be far less than that of outright war.

It is important to count the cost. In February 2024 it was reported that 315,000 Russian soldiers had died or been wounded fighting in Ukraine according to US defense sources.[13] Another source states that there are over half a million disabled Russians.[14] It is difficult to find information on Ukrainian deaths, although President Zelensky has reported 31,000,[15] but this is probably an underestimate. Then there are civilian casualties. There are huge economic costs, and the threat of wider war, even World War III. Violence compounds the pain of conflict, magnifies the sin.

It is important to recognize that there is significant resistance in Russia. There are currently 100,000 Russian conscientious objectors and deserters in neighboring Georgia,[16] and 20,000 Russian war protestors in prison.[17] In 2024 it was estimated that there are currently 250,000 Russian men outside the country avoiding mobilization.[18] This is all significant. Putin's Russian regime is vulnerable.

---

10. Heathershaw, "Theological Responses to the War against Ukraine," 56.
11. Heathershaw, "Theological Responses to the War against Ukraine," 57.
12. Heathershaw, "Theological Responses to the War against Ukraine," 61.
13. Robertson, "Ukrainian War Has Cost Russia."
14. Waterfield, "Cost of Putin's War in Ukraine."
15. BBC News, "Ukraine War."
16. Author's communication with Mixeli Elizbarasvili.
17. Sonne and Holder, "Russia's Brutal War Calculus."
18. Brett, "Numbers of Russian and Ukrainian Conscientious Objectors."

General David Richards, retired former British Chief of Defence Staff, and US General Mark Milley, as chair of the US Joint Chiefs of Staff, have both urged negotiations for peace in a costly, bogged-down war without an end in sight.[19]

REFLECTIONS

1. How is New Christian Realism different from Old Christian Realism? What are its strengths and weaknesses?
2. What are your feelings about 9/11? According to just war criteria, war should not be carried out as revenge nor be disproportionate. Also, civilians are to be immune.[20] In the War on Terror, have these just war criteria been followed?
3. John Heathershaw is critical of the just war position. He asserts it is not helpful politically, and lacks faith theologically. What do you think?
4. Was the War on Terror the war of a powerful empire lashing out at two weaker, poorer countries, Iraq and Afghanistan? Is it similar or different to how the Roman Empire acted?
5. What might be the role of Sermon on the Mount disciples in the Ukraine/Russia conflict? If you were a young man about to be conscripted into the Russian or Ukrainian army, would fleeing to another country be a faithful Christian response?

Prayer Thought

Holy Spirit, help us understand Jesus and how he might respond in our day to wars and terrorism. Jesus wept over Jerusalem because the people did not understand the things that made for peace. Help us understand what makes for peace in our times. Amen.

---

19. Rai, "British General Calls," 9.
20. Smock, *Religious Perspectives on War*, xiii–xiv.

32

Extraordinary Times

Polycrisis

> And you will hear of wars and rumors of wars; see that you are not alarmed; for this must take place, but the end is not yet. For nation will rise against nation, and kingdom against kingdom, and there will be famines and earthquakes in various places: all this is but the beginning of the birth pangs. (Matthew 24:6–8)

POLYCRISIS

We are in extraordinary times of polycrisis. It is like all of humanity is on the *Titanic*, and we face not one, but multiple icebergs ahead. The World Economic Forum recently published a survey of over 1,200 experts on the top ten global risks in ten years' time. Six of the ten global risks have to do with the environment, particularly climate change, seven if you include involuntary mass migration. Erosion of social cohesion, cybercrime/insecurity, and geopolitical confrontation are the last three risks.[1]

What else is going on? Populist politics are worrying, exemplified by the rise of far right parties in Europe and elsewhere, the crusading Christian right in the US, a bellicose Orthodox church in Russia, and the increasing fragility of democracy in many places. War is not mentioned by the World Economic Forum, but the largest land war in Europe since 1945 is ongoing

---

1. Torkington, "We're on the Brink of a 'Polycrisis.'"

in the Ukraine, and there are huge Middle East tensions centering currently on Israel/Palestine. Nuclear war could end everything. Cyberattacks are in the news regularly; that war has already begun. We should add neoliberal economics.

The quote from Matthew at the start of this chapter suggests he also knew about polycrisis in his Middle Eastern times—"all this is but the beginning of the birth pangs" of ever near possibilities of the kingdom of God. How can Sermon on the Mount disciples magnify hope in our serious polycrisis times?

DISCIPLESHIP IN EXTRAORDINARY POLYCRISIS TIMES

a) Economics and Spirit

Let us begin with our global, neoliberal economic system introduced by British prime minister Margaret Thatcher and US president Ronald Reagan in the 1980s. It is a system that rewards greed, that worships wealth, not God. It is fundamentally flawed. As Richard Wilkinson and Kate Pickett have convincingly demonstrated, unequal societies are dysfunctional and unhealthy places.[2] And as humans we cannot live by bread alone. Consuming more and more stuff does not satisfy the hole in our soul that only God's Spirit and healthy human relationships can.

We are called personally to live simply, in spiritual-material balance, not as consumers, but as stewards of life and the flourishing of the planet for the sake of everyone's children and grandchildren. For it is they who will reap our whirlwind.

Together we need to find and implement a better economic system. One example is "doughnut economics," pioneered by Oxford economist Kate Raworth. The outer rim of the doughnut symbolizes the ecological boundary, beyond which we are in trouble. The inner ring represents the social boundary beyond which people are in poverty and hurting. The actual dough represents a sustainable existence for the earth while meeting the needs of all humans. Raworth worked for the anti-poverty charity Oxfam for eleven years, as well as working in Africa and at the UN. She is an economist with a heart for economic justice for the poor, and profoundly understands planetary limits and our climate crisis. Her doughnut economics model offers seven new ways of thinking about the economy in

2. Wilkinson and Pickett, *Inner Level*.

our deeply troubled twenty-first century. It includes changing the goal from unsustainable GDP growth to human thriving within earth's capacity; ending inequality and redistributing not only income, but wealth, including enterprise, technology, knowledge, and power to create money; and creating to regenerate ecology, not degrade it.[3] Raworth's ideas, if implemented, might yet save us from the climate end times we face, the scandalous and widening gap between rich and poor, and the mayhem of mass migration, violence, and resource wars.

b) Thinking Globally and Acting Locally, Congregationally

As Christians, we are to think globally and act locally.

The Sermon on the Mount concludes with a global ethic, the Golden Rule. We remember "For God so loved the world . . . ,"[4] not just the Americas, Europe, Africa, or Asia. Worshipping our individual country is nationalism and a betrayal of our faith. All humans are made in God's image. We are wise when we are suspicious of the nation-state, its historical violence, and its potential for violence today. We remember that the Gospel of Matthew has no illusions about the Roman Empire.

Seeing all humans as God sees them—in great love—we are to act that out locally through congregational life. Being part of a Christian community is indispensable. To live in the neighborhood of where you worship is so helpful. My spouse and I live a five-minute walk from our small congregation, in the super-diverse city of Leicester, England.

Our congregation is part of Leicester and Leicestershire Citizens UK. Citizens UK is a community-organizing movement listening locally to those not normally heard. From our listening, for example, we have chosen to advocate locally for immigrant justice, better mental health support, racial justice in schools, and to address climate change. We raise our voices in civil, courteous, nonpartisan ways to the local council, and through members of parliament to national government. We are in partnership with other faiths, schools, the University of Leicester, and charities. Together we make a difference.

Historically, it is important to remember that British socialism owes more to British Christian Nonconformity than to Marxism. Left-wing Anglicans and working-class Catholics also helped significantly. In Britain, the

---

3. Raworth, *Doughnut Economics*, 27–31.
4. John 3:16.

free National Health Service is one triumph of this democratic Christian socialism. Jesus did not charge for healing.

A congregation learning, teaching, and practicing the Sermon on the Mount becomes creatively and faithfully nonconformist. We could do much more in this vein, and it is a reason for writing this book. It is in congregational life that we learn to walk the steps of the Beatitudes and become salt, light, and a city on a hill. We learn true worship: God and valuing our neighbor. We share generously through our offerings in ways that guard each one's dignity. We learn to fast, not only from food, but from those things that can distract us from Jesus' kingdom way. We pray personally and communally. We especially pray the Lord's Prayer so we can live it together.

c) Practicing Truth and Reconciliation

In Matthew 5:21–48 there are six discipleship commandments. All of them contribute to reconciliation. All of them move us from the fear/fight/flight/sex animal part of our brain to the frontal cortex that gives us the capacity to think wisely and make better decisions. These discipleship commandments apply in families, the congregation, neighborhoods, cities, nationally, and internationally. We start by learning and practicing locally.

Honesty in speech builds trust and authentic community. Censorship and propaganda can lead to violence. Truth is said to be the first casualty in war.[5] Sometimes politicians are dishonest. For example, according to *The Washington Post,* "In four years, President Trump made 30,573 false or misleading claims."[6] Honest history is important in order to understand what led to a particular war and the cost of that war. The West went to war against Iraq in 2003 based on a lie.

OPENNESS, RESEARCH, AND LEARNING

The Golden Rule summarizes the Sermon on the Mount with these words: "In everything do to others as you would have them do to you."[7] The Golden Rule also enables us to continue in the spirit of the Sermon on the Mount

---

5. Quoteresearcher, "Truth Is the First Casualty in War."
6. Kessler, "Trump Made."
7. Matthew 7:12.

to work out what we should do in new situations. It gives us a method for discerning what is the loving thing to do in those contexts. We are also to love God using all our mind, as well as heart and soul.[8] Thus, learning about history, sociology, psychology, primate evolution, peace studies, economics, and politics, as well as the scriptural text, is important to address our polycrisis times.

HOPE

There are many stories of hope told in this book, of people and movements that have taken the Sermon on the Mount seriously and shown the fruits of justice and peace. There are some other stories I want to mention in closing.

The World Council of Churches in 2011, after much discussion, moved from a just war to a just peace position. This includes addressing climate changes, economic justice, and human rights, as well as protecting human lives from war.[9] The Catholic Pax Christi movement is in talks with the Vatican to change the Church from just war to gospel nonviolence and just peace.[10] These are momentous possible changes. Imagine the Catholic Church becoming a peace church!

I am encouraged by people like Bill and Rosemary White and their courageous protest in the Just Stop Oil campaign. A retired Anglican priest, Bill has been arrested six times and imprisoned twice. Rosemary and Bill, such a loving couple, are motivated by the Sermon on the Mount as they protest on behalf of the welfare of future generations in our climate emergency times.[11]

Shane Claiborne and Tony Campolo's *Red Letter Revolution*[12] is a wonderful, grace-filled book describing the method of taking the words of Jesus seriously in the Gospels in discipleship formation. Red Letter Christians is a movement on both sides of the Atlantic that draws interest from high Anglicans to black Pentecostals.

---

8. Matthew 22:37.

9. World Council of Churches, *Just Peace Companion*.

10. See Dennis, ed., *Choosing Peace*, and Berger et al., *Advancing Nonviolence and Just Peace*.

11. White, "Sermon on the Mount."

12. Claiborne and Campolo, *Red Letter Revolution*.

I am encouraged by the work of Church and Peace, a European-wide ecumenical Christian peace network born out of the suffering and tragedy of World War II. At the heart of its vision is the Sermon on the Mount.[13]

The greatest hope centers in the story of Jesus. In the darkness and terror of Crucifixion Friday, Christians can have no illusions about sin, individually or collectively, no illusions about war and empires, no blindness to perils ahead. Yet in the early morning light of Easter Sunday, and an empty tomb, we can have hope.

It was brown women, in a brutally colonized land, who first discovered an empty tomb.

And it is committed Sermon on the Mount disciples today who are heralds of both hope and another way . . . "Thy kingdom come, thy will be done, on earth as it is in heaven."

---

13. Church and Peace, "Vision."

Bibliography

Acton, Lord. "Letter to Archbishop Mandell Creighton." April 5, 1887. http://history.hanover.edu/courses/excerpts/165acton.html.
Allison, Dale C., Jr. "Review of 'Ulrich Luz, *Matthew 1–7*: A Commentary, Minneapolis: Fortress, 2007.'" *Theology Today* 65/1 (April 2008) 133–34.
———. *The Sermon on the Mount: Inspiring the Moral Imagination*. New York: Crossroad, 1999.
Angell, Norman. *The Great Illusion*. London: Heinemann, 1913.
Arnold, Eberhard. *The Inner Life*. Vol. 3. Robertsbridge, UK: Plough, 2019.
Augustine. *The City of God against the Pagans*. Edited and translated by R. W. Dyson. Cambridge: Cambridge University Press, 1998. https://www.newadvent.org/fathers/120119.htm.
———. *Our Lord's Sermon on the Mount*, or *De sermon Domino in monte*. Translated by William Findlay. Revised and annotated by D. S. Shaff. https://biblehub.com/library/augustine/our_lords_sermon_on_the_mount/index.html.
Bainton, Roland H. *Christian Attitudes toward War and Peace: A Historic Survey and Critical Re-Evaluation*. Nashville: Abingdon, 1960.
Barrett, Clive. *Subversive Peacemakers: War Resistance 1914–1918: An Anglican Perspective*. Cambridge: Lutterworth, 2014.
BBC News. "Ukraine War: Zelensky Says 31,000 Troops Killed Since Russia's Full-Scale Invasion." February 25, 2024. https://www.bbc.co.uk/news/world-europe-68397525.
Bender, Harold S. "The Anabaptist Vision." *The Mennonite Quarterly Review* 18 (April 1944) 67–88. https://www.goshen.edu/mhl/Refocusing/d-av.htm.
Bennett, Scott H., and Charles F. Howlett. *Antiwar Dissent and Peace Activism in World War I America: A Documentary Reader*. Lincoln: University of Nebraska Press, 2014.
Benson, Lewis. "'That of God in Every Man': What Did George Fox Mean by It?" *Quaker Religious Thought* XII.2 (Spring 1970). http://qhpress.org/essays/togiem.html.
Berger, Rose Marie, Ken Butigan, Judy Coode, and Marie Dennis, eds. *Advancing Nonviolence and Just Peace in the Church and the World*. Brussels: Pax Christi International, 2020.
Betz, Hans Dieter. *The Sermon on the Mount: A Commentary on the Sermon on the Mount, including the Sermon on the Plain (Matthew 5:3—7:27 and Luke 6:20–49)*. Minneapolis: Fortress, 1995.
Betz, Hans Dieter, and William Schweiker. "Concerning Mountains and Morals: A Conversation about the Sermon on the Mount." *Criterion* (Spring/Summer 1997) 12–26.

Bibliography

Biblical Passages. "28 Which Explicitly Teach 'There is Only One God.'" https://www.monergism.com/28-biblical-passages-which-explicitly-teach-there-only-one-god.

Blomberg, Craig. "The Most Often Abused Verses in the Sermon on the Mount: And How to Treat Them Right." *Southwestern Journal of Theology* 46.3 (2004) 1–17.

Bonhoeffer, Dietrich. *The Cost of Discipleship.* Translated by R. H. Fuller. New York: Touchstone, 1995.

Book Launch. "Global Activism and Humanitarian Disarmament." Mary Kaldor response in launch of *Global Activism and Humanitarian Disarmament,* edited by Matthew Breay Bolton, Sarah Njeri, and Taylor Benjamin-Britton. London: Palgrave McMillan, 2020.

Borneman, Adam. "Barth on War, Peace, and Pacifism: A Primer." *Political Theology Network,* August 6, 2014. https://politicaltheology.com/barth-on-war-peace-and-pacifism-a-primer/#:~:text=At%20this%20point%2C%20we%20ought%20not%20to%20be,war%20should%20take%20the%20pacifist%20position%20seriously.%20.

Bouissou, Jean-Christophe. *Christ and Community.* Independence, MO: Herald, 1996.

Boulton, David. *Objection Overruled: Conscription and Conscience in the First World War.* Dent, Cumbria: Dales Historical Monographs, 2014.

Bredin, Mark. *Jesus, Revolutionary of the Poor: Matthew's Subversive Messiah.* Eugene, OR: Cascade, 2017.

Brett, Derek. "Numbers of Russian and Ukrainian Conscientious Objectors." Email to author, July 6 2024.

Brueggemann, Walter. "Jesus Acted Out the Alternative to Empire." *Sojourners,* June 22, 2018. https://sojo.net/articles/walter-brueggemann-jesus-acted-out-alternative-empire.

———. *Journey to the Common Good.* Louisville: Westminster John Knox, 2010.

———. *The Prophetic Imagination.* Minneapolis: Fortress, 2001.

Byaruhanga, Christopher. *Bishop Alfred Robert Tucker and the Establishment of the African Anglican Church.* Nairobi: Word Alive, 2008.

Cahill, Lisa Sowle. *Love Your Enemies: Discipleship, Pacifism and Just War Theory.* Minneapolis: Fortress, 1994.

Carroll, James. *Constantine's Sword: The Church and the Jews: A History.* New York: Houghton Mifflin, 2001.

Carter, Warren. *Matthew and the Margins: A Sociopolitical and Religious Reading.* Maryknoll, NY: Orbis, 2000.

Catterall, Peter. "The Distinctiveness of British Socialism? Religion and the Rise of Labour, c. 1900–39." In *The Foundations of the British Labour Party: Identities, Cultures and Perspectives, 1900-39,* edited by Matthew Worley, 131–52. Farnham: Ashgate, 2009.

Chadwick, Owen. *The Reformation.* London: Penguin, 1990.

Chávez-Nava, Citlalli, and Vanessa Codilla. "60 Years Ago Today: The Lunch Counter Sit-Ins That Changed History." UCLA College: Social Sciences; Institute for Research on Labor & Employment, February 20, 2020. https://irle.ucla.edu/2020/02/13/lunch_counter_sit-ins/.

Chenoweth, Erica. "The Future of Nonviolent Resistance." *Journal of Democracy* 31.3 (July 2020) 69–84.

Chenoweth, Erica, and Maria Stephan. *Why Civil Resistance Works: The Strategic Logic of Nonviolent Conflict.* New York: Columbia University Press, 2011.

Chmielewski, K. "Casualties of World War II." *Encyclopedia Britannica,* May 15, 2024. https://www.britannica.com/event/casualties-of-World-War-II-2231003.

Church and Peace. "Vision." https://www.church-and-peace.org/en/about-us/vision/.

Bibliography

Church of England. "Articles of Religion." https://www.churchofengland.org/prayer-and-worship/worship-texts-and-resources/book-common-prayer/articles-religion.

Claiborne, Shane, and Tony Campolo. *Red Letter Revolution: What If Jesus Really Meant What He Said?* Nashville: Thomas Nelson, 2012.

Clark, Christopher. *The Sleepwalkers: How Europe Went to War in 1914.* London: Allen Lane, 2012.

Clinton, Michael. "War against War: A Conversation with Michael Kazin." *Peace & Change* 42.4 (October 2017) 483–95.

Collins, John J. "Love Your Neighbor: How It Became the Golden Rule." Torah.com. https://ww.thetorah.com/article/love-your-neighbor-how-it-became-the-golden-rule.

Cooper, Sandi E. "Book Review." *Peace & Change* 44.4 (2019) 577–82.

"Costs of War Project." Watson Institute for International and Public Affairs, Brown University, Providence, RI, USA. https://watson.brown.edu/costsofwar/.

Crawford, Neta C. "Blood and Treasure: United States Budgetary Costs and Human Costs of 20 Years of War in Iraq and Syria, 2003–2023." Costs of War Project, Watson Institute for International and Public Affairs, Brown University, Providence, RI, USA. (March 15, 2023) 1–27. https://watson.brown.edu/costsofwar/files/cow/imce/papers/2023/Costs%20of%2020%20Years%20of%20Iraq%20War%20Crawford%2015%20March%202023%20final%203.21.2023.pdf.

Cruchley, Peter. "Turning Whiteness Purple." In *Deconstructing Whiteness, Empire and Mission,* edited by Anthony G. Reddie and Carol Troupe, 245–264. London: SCM, 2023.

Davies, W. D., and D. C. Allison Jr. *A Critical and Exegetical Commentary on the Gospel According to St Matthew. Volume 1: Introduction and Commentary on Matthew 1–7.* London: T & T Clark, 2004.

———. "Reflections on the Sermon on the Mount." *Scottish Journal of Theology* 44/3 (1991) 283–309.

Delgado, Richard, and Jean Stefancic. *Critical Race Theory: An Introduction.* 4th ed. New York: New York University Press, 2023.

Dennis, Marie, ed. *Choosing Peace: The Catholic Church Returns to Gospel Nonviolence.* Maryknoll, NY: Orbis, 2018.

Driver, John. *How Christians Made Peace with War.* Scottdale, PA: Herald, 1988.

Dueck, Abe J. "Sermon on the Mount." In *Global Anabaptist Mennonite Encyclopedia Online.* http://gameo.org/index.php?title=Sermon_on_the_Mount&oldid=143244.

Du Toit, Andrie B. "Revisiting the Sermon on the Mount: Some Major Issues." *Neotestamentica* 50.3 (2016) 59–91.

Dunbar-Ortiz, Roxanne. *An Indigenous Peoples' History of the United States.* Boston: Beacon, 2014.

Elizbarasvili, Mixeil. "German NGO Serving Russian and Ukrainian COs in Georgia." Email to author, February 2024.

Ellul, Jacques. *If You Are the Son of God: The Suffering and Temptations of Jesus.* Translated by Anne-Marie Andresson Hogg. Eugene, OR: Cascade, 2014.

Forest, Jim. "Climb the Ladder of the Beatitudes." *Salt of the Earth* (1997) 25–27.

———. *The Ladder of the Beatitudes.* Maryknoll, NY: Orbis, 1999.

Fox, George. *Journal of George Fox.* Rev. ed. Edited by John L. Nickalls. Cambridge: Cambridge University Press, 1952.

Bibliography

———. "Letter to Quaker Ministers from Prison in Launcheston, Cornwall." In *Quaker Faith and Practice*, 19.32. 5th ed. London: Yearly Meeting of the Religious Society of Friends (Quakers) in Britain, 2013.

Friedman, Maurice S. *Martin Buber: The Life of Dialogue*. New York: Harper & Row, 1960.

Friedman, Robert. "Anabaptism: 1955 Article." In *Global Anabaptist Mennonite Encyclopaedia Online*. https://gameo.org/index.php?title=Anabaptism.

Fromm, Erich. *The Fear of Freedom*. London: Routledge and Kegan Paul, 1942.

García, Mario T. *The Gospel of César Chávez: My Faith in Action*. Lanham, MD: Sheed and Ward, 2007.

Gill, Robin. *A Textbook of Christian Ethics*. 2nd ed. Edinburgh: T & T Clark, 1995.

Gingerich, Mark J. "Reinhold Niebuhr and the Sermon on the Mount in Dialogue with Stanley Hauerwas." MA thesis, Providence Theological Seminary, 2008.

Goldstone, Matthew. "The Structure of Matthew's Antitheses in Light of Early Jewish, Christian and Rabbinic Sources." *Journal for the Study of the New Testament* 40.2 (2017) 214–35.

Grant, Robert M. "The Sermon on the Mount in Early Christianity." *Semeia* 12 (1978) 215–31.

Greenman, Jeffrey P., Timothy Larsen, and Stephen R. Spencer, eds. *The Sermon on the Mount Through the Centuries: From the Early Church to John Paul II*. Grand Rapids: Brazos, 2007.

Guelich, Robert A. "Interpreting the Sermon on the Mount." *Interpretation: A Journal of Bible and Theology* 41.2 (1987) 117–30. https://journals.sagepub.com/doi/epdf/10.1177/002096438704100202.

———. *The Sermon on the Mount: Foundation for Understanding*. Dallas: Word, 1982.

Hagner, Donald A. "Ethics and the Sermon on the Mount." *Studia Theologica* 51.1 (1997) 44–59.

Hall, Douglas John. *The End of Christendom and the Future of Christianity*. Eugene, OR: Wipf and Stock, 2002.

Hallie, Philip. *Lest Innocent Blood Be Shed: The Story of the Village of Le Chambon and How Goodness Happened There*. New York: Harper & Row, 1979.

Halper, Jeff. *Decolonizing Israel, Liberating Palestine: Zionism, Settler Colonialism, and the Case for One Democratic State*. London: Pluto, 2021.

Hartrop, Joseph. "'Slay the Mad Dogs': How Luther Betrayed the Peasants' Revolt That He Inspired." *Christianity Today*, August 24, 2017. https://www.christiantoday.com/article/slay-the-mad-dogs-how-luther-betrayed-the-peasants-revolt-that-he-inspired/112430.htm.

Hauerwas, Stanley. "Living the Proclaimed Reign of God: A Sermon on the Sermon on the Mount." *Interpretation: A Journal of Bible and Theology* 47.2 (1993) 152–58.

Hay, David. *Exploring Inner Space: Is God Still Possible in the Twentieth Century?* London: Penguin, 1982.

Heathershaw, John. *Security After Christendom: Global Politics and Political Theology for Apocalyptic Time*. Eugene, OR: Cascade, 2024.

———. "Theological Responses to the War against Ukraine: A Reply to Joshua Searle." *Anabaptism Today* 5.2 (January 2024) 56–66.

Hecht, Mendy. "The 613 Commandments (Mitzvot)." *Chabad.org*. https://www.chabad.org/library/article_cdo/aid/756399/jewish/The-613-Commandments-Mitzvot.htm.

Heim, Mark. "The Sermon on the Mount: Ethic and Ethos." *Bangalore Theological Forum* 17.1 (1985) 65–82.

Bibliography

Heschel, Abraham. *The Prophets.* Perennial Classics. New York: HarperCollins, 2001.

Hobsbawn, E. J. *Nations and Nationalism Since 1780: Programme, Myth, Reality.* 2nd ed. Cambridge: Cambridge University Press, 1992.

Holland, Tom. *Rubicon: The Triumph and Tragedy of the Roman Republic.* London: Abacus, 2004.

Horsley, Richard. *Jesus and Empire: The Kingdom of God and the New World Disorder.* Minneapolis: Fortress, 2003.

Ingle, H. Larry. *First Among Friends: George Fox and the Creation of Quakerism.* Oxford: Oxford University Press, 1994.

Instone-Brewer, David. *Divorce and Remarriage in the Bible.* Milton Keynes: Paternoster, 2011.

Iraq Body Count. https://www.iraqbodycount.org.

Jackson, Ashley. *The British Empire: A Very Short Introduction.* Oxford: Oxford University Press, 2013.

Katz, Mandy. "Do We Divide the Holiest Holy City?" *Moment Magazine,* March/April 2008, 1–8. https://momentmag.com/do-we-divide-the-holiest-holy-city/.

Keegan, John. *The First World War.* London: Hutchinson, 1998.

Kertzer, David I. *The Pope at War: The Secret History of Pius XII, Mussolini, and Hitler.* Oxford: Oxford University Press, 2022.

Kessler, Glen, "Trump Made 30,573 False or Misleading Claims as President. Nearly Half Came in His Final Year." *Washington Post,* January 23, 2021. https://www.washingtonpost.com/politics/how-fact-checker-tracked-trump-claims/2021/01/23/ad04b69a-5c1d-11eb-a976-bad6431e03e2_story.html.

King, Coretta Scott. *The Words of Martin Luther King Jr.* New York: Newmarket, 1987.

King, Martin Luther, Jr. "Drum Major Instinct Speech: 'Say That I Was a Drum Major for Justice.'" Ebenezer Baptist Church, Atlanta, February 4, 1968. https://newyorktheater.me/2022/01/17/martin-luther-king-jr-drum-major-instinct-speech-say-that-i-was-a-drum-major-for-justice/.

———. "'The Negro Is Your Brother' (Letter from a Birmingham Jail)." *The Atlantic Monthly* 212.2 (August 1963) 78–88. https://www.csuchico.edu/iege/_assets/documents/susi-letter-from-birmingham-jail.pdf.

———. "Out of the Long Night." *Gospel Messenger/Church of the Brethren* (February 8, 1958) 3–4, 13–15. https://archive.org/details/gospelmessengerv107mors/page/n165/mode/2up.

———. *Strength to Love.* Glasgow: Collins/Fontana, 1969.

———. *Where Do We Go from Here: Chaos or Community?* Boston: Beacon, 2010.

King, Mary Elizabeth. "Why We Need Sharp's Dictionary." Waging Nonviolence, April 9, 2012. https://wagingnonviolence.org/2012/04/why-we-need-sharps-dictionary/.

Kirby, Robert I. "The Sermon on the Mount Site: The Epistle of James, Applying the Sermon on the Mount?" https://www.sermononthemount.org.uk/Bible/James.html.

Kissinger, Warren S. *The Sermon on the Mount: A History of Interpretation and Bibliography.* Metuchen, NJ: Scarecrow Press and the American Theological Library Association, 1975.

Kloppenborg, John S. *Q, the Earliest Gospel: An Introduction to the Original Stories and Sayings of Jesus.* Louisville: Westminster John Knox, 2008.

Kraybill, Donald B., Steven Nolt, and David Weaver-Zercher. *Amish Grace: How Forgiveness Transcended Tragedy.* San Francisco: Jossey-Bass, 2007.

Bibliography

Kreider, Alan. *The Patient Ferment of the Early Church: The Improbable Rise of Christianity in the Roman Empire*. Grand Rapids: Baker Academic, 2016.

Küng, Hans, and Karl-Josef Kuschel. *A Global Ethic: The Declaration of the Parliament of the World's Religions*. Special ed. New York: Continuum, 2006.

Landau, Ronnie S. *The Nazi Holocaust*. London: I. B. Taurus, 1992.

Lapide, Pinchas. *The Sermon on the Mount: Utopia or Program for Action?* Translated by Arlene Swidler. Maryknoll, NY: Orbis, 1986.

Layton, Julia. "Top 10 Heads That Rolled During the Reign of Henry VIII." How Stuff Works. https://history.howstuffworks.com/historical-figures/10-henry-viii-executions.htm#pt9.

Luther, Martin. "Against the Robbing and Murdering Hordes of Peasants." In *Luther's Works*, vol. 46, translated by Charles M. Jacobs and edited by Robert C. Schultz, 45–55. Philadelphia: Fortress, 1967.

———. "On the Jews and Their Lies." In *Luther's Works*, vol. 47, translated by Martin H. Bertram and edited by Franklin Sherman, 121–306. Philadelphia: Fortress, 1971.

Luz, Ulrich. *Matthew 1–7*. Hermeneia: A Critical And Historical Commentary On The Bible. Translated by James E. Crouch. Minneapolis: Fortress, 2007.

Machinek, Marian. "Gerhard Lohfink's Interpretative Key to the Sermon on the Mount." *Verbum Vitae* 39.4 (2021) 1335–55.

Marans, Nick E. "On Luther and His Lies." *The Christian Century*, October 25, 2017. https://www.christiancentury.org/article/critical-essay/on-luther-and-lies.

Marcus, Joel. "The Enigma of the Antitheses." *New Testament Studies* 69 (2023) 121–37. https:// doi.org/10.1017/S0028688522000352.

Mattia, Joan Plubell. *Walking the Rift: Idealism and Imperialism in East Africa; Alfred Robert Tucker (1890–1911)*. Eugene, OR: Pickwick, 2017.

Megoran, Nick. *Warlike Christians in an Age of Violence*. Eugene, OR: Cascade, 2017.

Monbiot, George. "The World According to Jason." *The Guardian Weekly*, May 10, 2024, 35–39.

Murray, Stuart. *Post-Christendom: Church and Mission in a Strange New World*. 2nd ed. Eugene, OR: Cascade, 2018.

Myhrvold-Hanssen, Thomas L. "Democracy, News Media, and Famine Prevention: Amartya Sen and The Bihar Famine of 1966-67." University of Pennsylvania—School of Arts & Science, June 2003. https://www.sas.upenn.edu/%7Edludden/BIHAR1967counterSen.pdf.

My Jewish Learning. "Teshuvah, or Repentance." https://www.myjewishlearning.com/article/repentance/.

Nation, Mark Thiessen, Anthony G. Siegrist, and Daniel P. Umbel. *Bonhoeffer the Assassin? Challenging the Myth, Recovering His Call to Peacemaking*. Grand Rapids: Baker Academic, 2013.

Nation, Mark Thiessen. *Discipleship in a World Full of Nazis: Recovering the True Legacy of Dietrich Bonhoeffer*. Eugene, OR: Cascade, 2022.

Nation, Mark Thiessen, and Stanley Hauerwas. "'A Pacifist and Enemy of the State': Dietrich Bonhoeffer's Journey to Nonviolence." *ABC Religion and Ethics*, April 19, 2018, updated January 30, 2019. https://www.abc.net.au/religion/a-pacifist-and-enemy-of-the-state-bonhoeffers-journey-to-nonviol/10094798.

Nauert, Charles G. "Review of Tore Meistad, *Martin Luther and John Wesley on the Sermon on the Mount*." Lanham, MD: Scarecrow, 1999." *Church History* 70.3 (2001) 572.

Bibliography

Niebuhr, Reinhold. *Moral Man and Immoral Society: A Study in Ethics and Politics.* New York: Charles Scribner's Sons, 1932.

Noll, Mark. "John Wesley." In *The Sermon on the Mount Through the Centuries: From the Early Church to John Paul II*, edited by Jeffrey P. Greenman, Timothy Larsen, and Stephen R. Spencer, 153–80. Grand Rapids: Brazos, 2007.

Nugent, John C. "A Yoderian Rejoinder to Peter J. Leithart's Defending Constantine." In *Constantine Revisited: Leithart, Yoder, and the Constantine Debate,* edited by John D. Roth, 1–24. Eugene, OR: Pickwick, 2013.

Orosco, José-Antonio. *Cesar Chavez and the Common Sense of Nonviolence.* Albuquerque: University of New Mexico Press, 2008.

Palmer, W. T. *In Lakeland Dells and Fells.* London: Chatto & Windus, 1903.

Paul, Garrett E. "Jesus' Ethic of Perfection." *Christian Century* 113 (March 6, 1996) 270–74.

Pearce, Cyril. *Communities of Resistance: Conscience and Dissent in Britain during the First World War.* London: Francis Boutle, 2020.

Poverty and Justice Bible (NRSV). Swindon UK: The United Bible Societies, 2013.

"Psychological Inflexibility: An ACT View of Suffering and Failure to Thrive." *Association for Contextual Behavioral Science.* https://contextualscience.org/about_act.

Puri, Kavita. "Three Million." BBC Radio 4 and World Service, February 12, 2024. https://www.bbc.co.uk/mediacentre/2024/documentary-series-three-million-radio-4-world-service.

"Quakers and the Nobel Peace Prize." https://quakernobel.org.

Quaker Faith and Practice. 5th ed. London: Yearly Meeting of the Religious Society of Friends (Quakers) in Britain, 2013. https://qfp.quaker.org.uk/chapter/19/.

Quoteresearcher. "Truth Is the First Casualty in War." *Quote Investigator,* April 11, 2020. https://quoteinvestigator.com/2020/04/11/casualty/.

Rai, Milan. "British general calls for Ukraine negotiations: 'peace for land.'" *Peace News,* April–May 2024, 9.

Rajkumar, Peniel. "Postcolonialism and Re-stor(y)ing the Ecumenical Movement." In *Deconstructing Whiteness, Empire and Mission,* edited by Anthony G. Reddie and Carol Troupe, 102–19. London: SCM, 2023.

Rasmussen, Larry. *Reinhold Niebuhr: Theologian of Public Life.* London: Collins, 1989.

Rathbone, James. "Happily Ever After—The Science of Happiness." *Keystone Psychology,* European Peace Colloquy, Dunfield, 2024.

Raworth, Kate. *Doughnut Economics: Seven Ways to Think Like a 21st Century Economist.* New York: Random House Business, 2018.

Rickerman, Sally. "Twentieth Century Organizations Founded by Individual Quakers, or Groups of Quakers or Quakers in Other Organizations," Philadelphia Yearly Meeting—Advancement and Outreach—R6.

Richards, Leyton. *The Christian's Alternative to War.* 4th ed. London: Student Christian Movement, 1930.

Riddell, Rebecca, et al. "Inequality Inc." *Oxfam,* January 15, 2024. https://www.oxfam.org/en/research/inequality-inc.

Rieder, Rem. "Checking the Facts in the World of Trump." *FactCheck.org,* November 25, 2020. https://www.factcheck.org/2020/11/checking-the-facts-in-the-world-of-trump/.

Bibliography

Rigoli, John I., and Diane Cummings. "The Vatican Chronicles—The Mystery of Julia Episcopa." May 4, 2017 http://vaticanchronicles.com/persecution-in-the-early-church-religionfacts/.

Robertson, Noah. "Ukrainian War Has Cost Russia up to $211 Billion, Pentagon Says." *Defense News*, February 16, 2024. https://www.defensenews.com/pentagon/2024/02/16/ukraine-war-has-cost-russia-up-to-211-billion-pentagon-says/.

Rodger, Alex R. *Developing Moral Community in a Pluralistic School Setting*. Aberdeen: Gordon Cook Foundation, 1996.

Roser, Max. "The Spanish Flu: The Global Impact of the Largest Influenza Pandemic in History." https://ourworldindata.org/spanish-flu-largest-influenza-pandemic-in-history.

Sanghera, Sathnam. *Empireworld: How British Imperialism Has Shaped the Globe*. Dublin: Penguin Random House UK, 2024.

"Schleitheim Confession." 1527. https://www.anabaptists.org/history/the-schleitheim-confession.html.

Schrock, David, "3 Ways to Misread the Sermon on the Mount." *Southern Seminary*, June 22, 2018. https://equip.sbts.edu/article/3-ways-misread-sermon-mount/.

Schumacher, Ernst F. *Small Is Beautiful: Economics as if People Mattered*. New York: Harper and Row, 1975.

Sharp, Gene. *The Politics of Nonviolent Action. Part One: Power and Struggle*. Boston: Porter Sargeant, 1973.

Shepherd, Arthur P. *Tucker of Uganda: Artist and Apostle 1894-1914*. London: Student Christian Movement, 1929.

Shuchat, Chaya. "Eight Degrees of Giving." Chabad.org. https://www.chabad.org/library/article_edo/aid/256321/jewish/Eight-Degrees-of-Giving.htm.

Sider, Ronald J., ed. *The Early Church on Killing: A Comprehensive Sourcebook on War, Abortion, and Capital Punishment*. Grand Rapids: Baker Academic, 2012.

Smock, David R. *Religious Perspectives on War: Christian, Muslim, and Jewish Attitudes Toward Force After the Gulf War*. Washington, DC: United States Institute of Peace, 1992.

Solzhenitsyn, Aleksandr I. *The Gulag Archipelago 1918-1956*. Goodreads Quotes. https://www.goodreads.com/author/quotes/10420.Aleksandr_Solzhenitsyn.

Sonne, Paul, and Josh Holder. "Russia's Brutal War Calculus." *New York Times*, February 23, 2024. https://www.nytimes.com/interactive/2024/02/24/world/europe/russia-war-calculus.html.

"Source List and Detailed Death Tolls for the Primary Megadeaths of the Twentieth Century." http://necrometrics.com/20c5m.htm#WW1.

Spencer, Stephen R. "John Calvin." In *The Sermon on the Mount Through the Centuries: From the Early Church to John Paul II*, edited by Jeffrey P. Greenman, Timothy Larsen, and Stephen R. Spencer, 129–52. Grand Rapids: Brazos, 2007.

Standing, Guy. *Plunder of the Commons: A Manifesto for Sharing Public Wealth*. London: Penguin, 2019.

Stassen, Glen H. "The Fourteen Triads of the Sermon on the Mount (Matthew 5:21–7:12)." *Journal of Biblical Literature* 122 (2003) 267–308.

Stephenson, John R. "The Two Governments and the Two Kingdoms in Luther's Thought." *Scottish Journal of Theology* 34 (1981) 321–37.

Bibliography

Sterling, Hamish. "Reinhold Niebuhr and the Nuclear Dilemma: Conceptualising the Cold War." *Journal of American History and Politics* 3.1 (2020) 17–34.

Stoltzfus, Duane C. S. *Pacifists in Chains: The Persecution of Hutterites during the Great War*. Baltimore: John Hopkins University Press, 2013.

Subrahmanyan, P. T. "Mahatma Gandhi and the Sermon on the Mount." *Gandhi Marg*, 39.1 (April–June 2017) 97–107. https://www.mkgandhi.org/articles/mahatma-gandhi-and-sermon-on-the-mount.html.

Swancutt, Diana M. "'Forgive Us Our Debts': Jubilee prays the Lord's Prayer." *Review and Expositor* 118.4 (2021) 460–67.

Swartley, Willard M. *Covenant of Peace: The Missing Peace*. Grand Rapids: Eerdmans, 2006.

Tolstoy, Leo. *The Kingdom of God is Within You: Christianity Not as a Mystic Religion But as a New Theory of Life*. Translated by Constance Garnett. Lincoln: University of Nebraska Press, 1984.

Torkington, Simon. "We're on the Brink of a 'Polycrisis'—How Worried Should We Be?" *World Economic Forum*, January 13, 2023. https://www.weforum.org/agenda/2023/01/polycrisis-global-risks-report-cost-of-living/.

Understanding Humanism. "The Golden Rule." https://understandinghumanism.org.uk/wp-content/uploads/2021/10/Golden-Rule.pdf.

Waterfield, Bruno. "Cost of Putin's War in Ukraine Is Half a Million Disabled Russians." *The Times & The Sunday Times*, April 4, 2024. https://www.thetimes.co.uk/article/vladimir-putin-cost-war-ukraine-disabled-men-russia-8666wj9nb.

Weaver, Dorothy Jean. *The Irony of Power: The Politics of God within Matthew's Narrative*. Eugene, OR: Pickwick, 2017.

Wesley, John. Sermon 22. "Upon our Lord's Sermon on the Mount." Discourse 2.III.18. https://www.ccel.org/ccel/wesley/sermons.v.xxii.html.

"What Game Theory Reveals About Life, The Universe, and Everything." YouTube. https://www.youtube.com/watch?v=mScpHTIi-kM&t=502s.

White, Rosemary. "Reflection notes on the Sermon on the Mount." Interview with author. September 9, 2022.

Wikipedia. "Air Raids on Japan." https://en.wikipedia.org/wiki/Air_raids_on_Japan.

———. "Golden Rule." https://en.wikipedia.org/wiki/Golden_Rule.

———. "Holocaust Victims." https://en.wikipedia.org/wiki/Holocaust_victims.

———. "Institute of Rural Reconstruction." https://en.wikipedia.org/wiki/International_Institute_of_Rural_Reconstruction.

———. "Pope Benedict XV." https://en.wikipedia.org/wiki/Pope_Benedict_XV.

———. "Y. C. James Yen." https://en.wikipedia.org/wiki/Y._C._James_Yen.

Wilken, Robert Louis. "Augustine." In *The Sermon on the Mount Through the Centuries: From the Early Church to John Paul II*. Edited by Jeffrey P. Greenman, Timothy Larsen, and Stephen R. Spencer, 43–57. Grand Rapids: Brazos, 2007.

Wilkinson, Richard, and Kate Pickett. *The Inner Level: How More Equal Societies Reduce Stress, Restore Sanity and Improve Everyone's Well-being*. London: Allen Lane, 2018.

Wink, Walter. *Engaging the Powers: Discernment and Resistance in a World of Domination*. Minneapolis: Fortress, 1992.

World Council of Churches. *Just Peace Companion*. 2nd ed. Geneva: WCC, 2012.

World History Encyclopedia. "Allied Bombing of Germany." https://www.worldhistory.org/article/2430/allied-bombing-of-germany/.

Bibliography

Yang, S-A. "Sermon on the Mount/Plain." In *Dictionary of Jesus and the Gospels*, 2nd ed., 845–55. Nottingham: InterVarsity, 2013.

Yen, Y. C. James. AZQuotes. https://www.azquotes.com/quote/1034632.

Yoder, Anne M. "World War I Conscientious Objector Data Base." Swarthmore College Peace Collection. http://www.swarthmore.edu/Library/peace/conscientiousobjection/WWI.COs.coverpage.htm.

Yoder, John H. *Christian Attitudes to War, Peace and Revolution*. Goshen, IN: Goshen Biblical Seminary, 1981.

Yoder, Perry B. *Shalom: The Bible's Word for Salvation, Justice and Peace*. Nappanee, IN: Evangel, 1987.

www.ingramcontent.com/pod-product-compliance
Lightning Source LLC
Chambersburg PA
CBHW021914180426
43198CB00035B/544